ARCHITECTURAL DESIGN

GUEST-EDITED BY
PIA EDNIE-BROWN,
MARK BURRY AND
ANDREW BURROW

THE INNOVATION IMPERATIVE

ARCHITECTURES OF VITALITY

01|2013

ARCHITECTURAL DESIGN
JANUARY/FEBRUARY 2013
ISSN 0003-8504

PROFILE NO 221
ISBN 978-1119-978657

ARCHITECTURAL DESIGN

GUEST-EDITED BY
PIA EDNIE-BROWN,
MARK BURRY AND
ANDREW BURROW

THE INNOVATION IMPERATIVE: ARCHITECTURES OF VITALITY

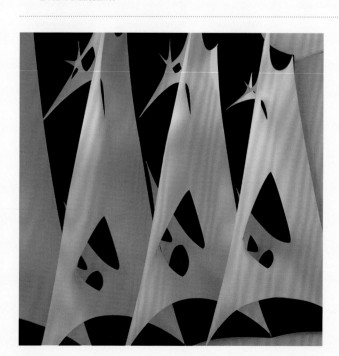

56

70

62

'Vitality, the state of being vigorous and active, invokes notions of the seed that … grows into a plant yielding future seeds. Conceptual and technological inventions only become innovations when the conditions are right … – windborne seeds blown to new gardens.'
— *Pia Ednie-Brown, Mark Burry and Andrew Burrow*

ARCHITECTURAL DESIGN
JANUARY/FEBRUARY 2013
PROFILE NO 221

Editorial Offices
John Wiley & Sons
25 John Street
London
WC1N 2BS
UK

T: +44 (0)20 8326 3800

Editor
Helen Castle

Managing Editor (Freelance)
Caroline Ellerby

Production Editor
Elizabeth Gongde

Prepress
Artmedia, London

Art Direction and Design
CHK Design:
Christian Küsters
Sophie Troppmair

Printed in Italy by Conti Tipocolor

Sponsorship/advertising
Faith Pidduck/Wayne Frost
T: +44 (0)1243 770254
E: fpidduck@wiley.co.uk

Subscribe to Δ

Δ is published bimonthly and is
available to purchase on both a
subscription basis and as individual
volumes at the following prices.

Prices
Individual copies: £24.99 / US$45
Individual issues on Δ App
for iPad: £9.99 / US$13.99
Mailing fees for print may apply

Annual Subscription Rates
Student: £75 / US$117 print only
Personal: £120 / US$189 print and
iPad access
Institutional: £212 / US$398 print
or online
Institutional: £244 / US$457
combined print and online
6-issue subscription on Δ App
for iPad: £44.99 / US$64.99

Subscription Offices UK
John Wiley & Sons Ltd
Journals Administration Department
1 Oldlands Way, Bognor Regis
West Sussex, PO22 9SA, UK
T: +44 (0)1243 843 272
F: +44 (0)1243 843 232
E: cs-journals@wiley.co.uk

Print ISSN: 0003-8504
Online ISSN: 1554-2769

Prices are for six issues and include
postage and handling charges.
Individual-rate subscriptions must be
paid by personal cheque or credit card.
Individual-rate subscriptions may not
be resold or used as library copies.

All prices are subject to change
without notice.

Rights and Permissions
Requests to the Publisher should be
addressed to:
Permissions Department
John Wiley & Sons Ltd
The Atrium
Southern Gate
Chichester
West Sussex PO19 8SQ
UK

F: +44 (0)1243 770 620
E: permreq@wiley.co.uk

Front cover: The Nervous System of the World
© Edited and redrawn by Michael Weinstock
from Global Map of Accessibility, Joint Research
Centre, Global Environment Monitoring Unit,
European Commission for the World Bank's
2009 report 'Reshaping Economic Geography'.

Inside front cover: Minifie van Schaik (MvS),
Cloudnets I and II, 2008. © Minifie van Schaik
Architects/Paul Minifie

Erratum
Architectural Design (Δ) would like to apologise
for the spelling mistakes in *City Catalyst* (Vol 82,
No 5), p 28. In the standfirst, the development of
suppliers should be spelled 'Vendorville' and the
contributor's first name 'Jesse LeCavalier'.

Innovation has become the golden goose of the 21st century, as expressed by Barack Obama in his presidential victory speech on 7 November 2012 in Chicago: 'We want our kids to grow up in a country ... that lives up to its legacy as the global leader in technology and discovery and innovation with all of the good jobs and new businesses that follow.'[1] For stagnating developed economies, innovation remains the great white hope – the essential stimulus to ongoing prosperity sought through entrepreneurship, Internet startups and biotech, software and hardware companies.

For the practice of architecture, no simple equation exists between innovation and commercial success. Most truly innovative designers are not purely motivated by wealth. In contemporary architecture, innovation is a life force. Architecture thrives off the impulse to innovate. At a day-to-day level it is what elevates architecture beyond mere building production, and the original and analytical thinking that makes clients come back for more, while making us reach for our smart phone to see the latest architectural project on Facebook. What guest-editors Pia Ednie-Brown, Mark Burry and Andrew Burrow bring to this issue is a new clarity and tautness to the definition of 'innovation' in architecture. Their subtitle for the publication – 'architectures of vitality' – chimes with notions of emergence, but also of architecture as a collective practice in tune with current processes and cultural shifts.

What drew ⟁ to the theme of this issue – aside from the opportunity to work with key members of the Spatial Information Architecture Laboratory (SIAL) at RMIT in Melbourne – was its timeliness. The innovation imperative today requires a greater intensity than it might have 50 years ago. As the guest-editors state in their introduction: 'The urge to examine innovation more closely – and in relation to architecture in particular – is inflected by the broadly defining conditions of rapid change we find ourselves in.' A new level of ingenuity is called upon not only to keep in step with shifts in technology, but also to retain architecture's relevance at a time of economic, social, environmental and political change. ⟁

Note
1. For the full text of Barack Obama's victory speech, see: www.guardian.co.uk/world/2012/nov/07/barack-obama-speech-full-text.

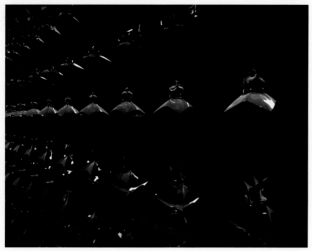

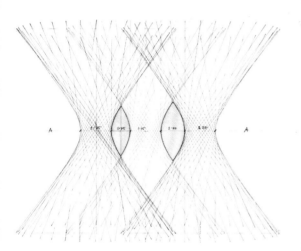

Poots de les celumnes con inclinación de elipse a 6°

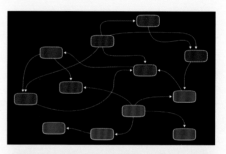

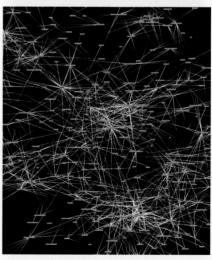

Pia Ednie-Brown, Mock-up for a latex skin installation, Melbourne, 2003
top centre: This latex skin was painted onto and peeled off a tiled shower recess. It was produced as part of the experimentation and mock-up process for an interaction installation then under development.

Pia Ednie-Brown, *Plastic Futures*, State of Design Festival, Melbourne, 2009
top right: *Plastic Futures* explored the intersections of bio-art and contemporary field-based design practices in the context of 'speculative futures'. Working with a group of RMIT postgraduate architecture and fashion students, the project included a workshop at SymbioticA (University of Western Australia) and the site of Lake Clifton in Western Australia, where biotechnical laboratory processes, ancient biological histories and contemporary planning and conservation problems were explored. The workshop informed and inflected the production of an ethically loaded speculative future scenario for the exhibition and installation in Melbourne.

Mark Burry, *The Third Policeman*, Black Air, 1998/2010
top left: From Mark Burry, *Scripting Cultures, Architectural Design and Programming*, John Wiley & Sons (London), 2010.

Antoni Gaudí, Sagrada Família Basilica, Barcelona, 1882–
above: Horizontal section across a window design, 1980. Drawing by Mark Burry.

Andrew Burrow, Diagram of a rooted oriented graph, 2011
above top: The oriented and rooted graph proved to be a strong model for navigation in collaboratively edited hypertexts at SIAL. In this small fragment, the roots are the nodes with no inward-pointing edges; they represent entry points in a shared text, but these are not walled gardens, as many nodes are reachable from either root node.

Andrew Burrow, Snapshot of albCorpus wiki, 2009
above bottom: The dense interconnections of a hypertext comprehensively recording digital work practices during a period of intense software development.

Pia Ednie-Brown, Mark Burry and Andrew Burrow are founding members of the Spatial Information Architecture Laboratory (SIAL) in the School of Architecture and Design at RMIT University in Melbourne, Australia. They have led the establishment of a holistic spatial design research environment dedicated to almost all aspects of contemporary spatial design activity, a facility for innovation in transdisciplinary design research and education. SIAL embraces a broad range of investigative modes, involving both highly speculative and industry-linked projects. Researchers are engaged in a wide variety of projects that collaboratively disturb artificial distinctions between the physical and virtual, digital and analogue, scientific and artistic, instrumental and philosophical.

This issue of ⊿ is an outcome of a research project supported by the Australian Research Council (2009–11). The project sought to re-theorise innovation for contemporary design practices in terms of coupled ethical and aesthetic concerns therein, focusing on case studies from digital architecture, the biological arts and their intersections. Chief investigators were Pia Ednie-Brown, Mark Burry, Andrew Burrow and Oron Catts of SymbioticA.

Pia Ednie-Brown is a designer, theorist and educator with creative research practice Onomatopoeia. She is an associate professor at RMIT University, based in both the Architecture programme and SIAL. Her doctoral research, 'The Aesthetics of Emergence' (2007) articulated new ways of understanding architectural composition in the context of processually and behaviourally oriented creative production. Her research continues to explore the implications of new technologies in design, relations between composition, diagramming, embodiment and affect, and ethics and aesthetics. Her book *Plastic Green: Designing for Environmental Transformation* (RMIT University Press, 2009) is an outcome of one of her creative research projects involving multiple disciplines across the arts and science. Recent creative projects have included *Plastic Futures*, exhibited at the Victoria State of Design Festival (2009) and *Change Room* at the 2012 Biennale of Sydney as part of Erin Manning's participatory work, *Stitching Time*.

Professor Mark Burry has published internationally on three main themes: the life and work of the architect Antoni Gaudí in Barcelona, putting theory into practice with regard to 'challenging' architecture, and transdisciplinary design education and practice. His research focuses on the broader issues of design, construction and the use of computers in design theory and practice. He is the founding director of RMIT University's Design Research Institute (DRI) and SIAL. The DRI positions the role of design research as an 'explorer and tester of design options' focusing on the challenges of urbanisation and growing cities of the future. Since 1979, Burry has been a key member of the Sagrada Família Basilica design team based on site in Barcelona. For over three decades he has been helping untangle the mysteries of Gaudí's compositional strategies for his greatest work in order to inform the ongoing construction.

Andrew Burrow is a senior research fellow at SIAL. His research interests concern computational accounts in design. He has completed a PhD on the subject, demonstrating the foundational algorithms for a class of design-space explorers that operate over information orderings. Recognising that the social context of the designer is crucial to computer-aided design, he has also worked on tools to negotiate access to resources to assist in the early stages of team development, and to explicitly consider the performative aspects of communication. His current research concerns collective map-building as a means to negotiate representations of expertise. ⊿

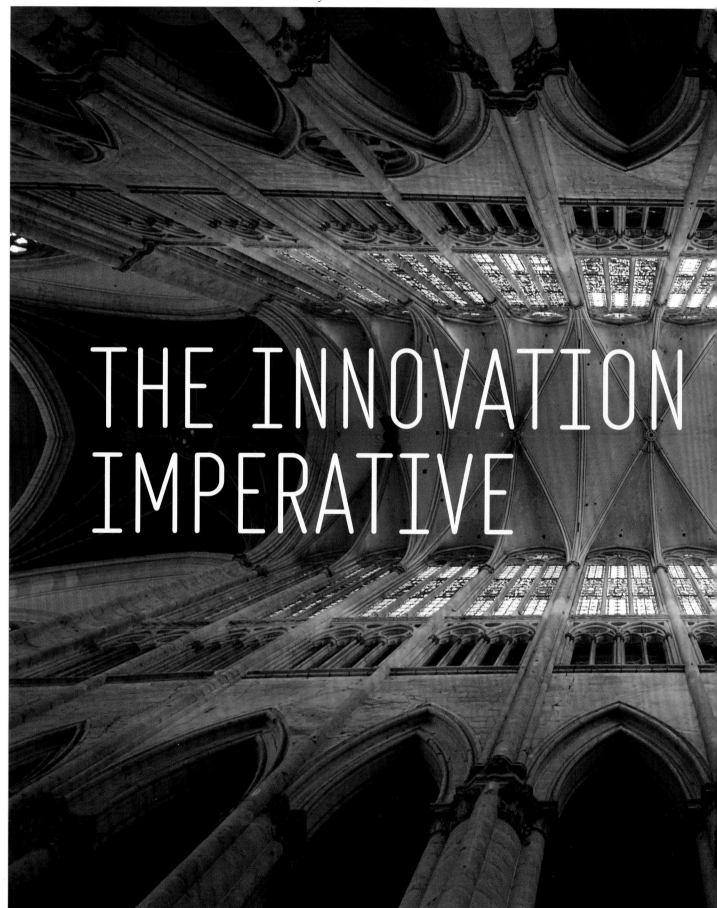

THE INNOVATION IMPERATIVE

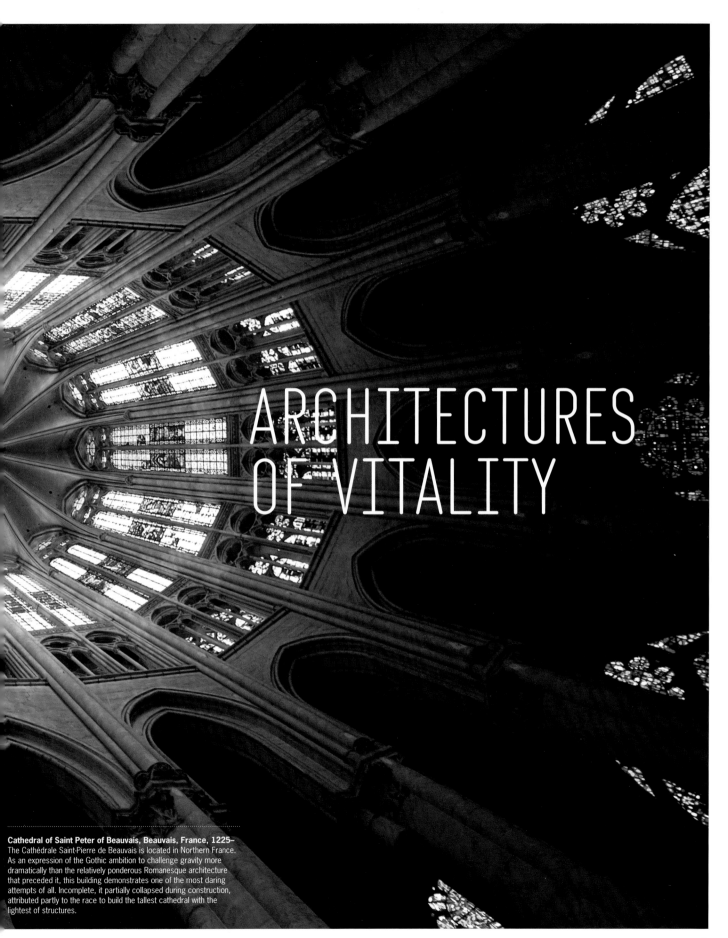

ARCHITECTURES OF VITALITY

Innovation points to an attitude and an ethos that might be summarised in the simple directive of: 'make a difference'.

The role of △, in general, includes offering an index of innovation – cumulatively gathering a history of the new and mapping tectonic movements of the architectural landscape. For this issue we have undertaken the task of focusing on architectural innovation directly. Such a project presents a very immediate problem: so ubiquitous has 'innovation' become as a word that its meaning has been blurred by its very omnipresence or 'everywhere-ness'. Approaching the topic is like stepping into a space of infinite echo and struggling to locate or pin down the source – the sound of 'innovation' rebounding all around us, but without clear meaning. Perhaps the innovation imperative has become 'a kind of Warholian dream, [where] every echo has become an original artwork',[1] as Mark Wigley once put it. However, simply dismissing the echo as 'nothing new' risks missing the point.

In the continuum that is the cyclical nature of history, the innovations that have been at the forefront of public consciousness are those that disrupt the status quo, thereby signalling progress. As bold new forward steps beyond the known, architectural movements, such as Modernism, are often the more conspicuous for their advancement through a collective will – a distributed leadership more often than a single leader. As movements, the collective will arguably sits at a higher level than the names and reputations of the individual genii at its vanguard. Regardless of the singularity (as blips in the continuum), whatever unknown political innovations afforded Stonehenge and the Pyramids, or the cultural innovation springing from a classical language of architecture, the Gothic sanitisers of Romanesque's rawness, the humanists at the foundation of the Renaissance, the technical evangelists emanating from the Industrial Revolution, all point to an innovation imperative as a longstanding condition. This issue therefore sits within the multi-millennial tradition of progressive architecture, but has here-now qualities that identify this latest iteration from all that has gone before.

Innovation points to an attitude and an ethos that might be summarised in the simple directive of: 'make a difference'. While not 'morally neutral', innovation is surely about creating positive impact and adding value, redirecting collective activity and changing the world in some way for the better. But such comfortable assertions only accentuate the troubling, echoic vagueness of the topic in relation to architecture, where every architectural project makes a difference, however slight. Everything 'designed' is somehow new and different, is it not? There are gestures that clearly make bigger and more significant differences than others – but where do you draw the line between one difference and another, between what is innovative and what is not?

We have decided to address these issues by approaching innovation through a slightly alternative emphasis: as an activity that generates vitality. This gives an experiential edge to the notion, allowing us to focus less on the 'new' or on what innovation is per se, than on what we do, how we do it, and the value it offers to our individual and collective experience (as a kind of raison d'être). By attending to some of the tactics and strategies that can be found across a range of innovative practices, our intention is to highlight practice over product, and provoke questions about the ethical dimensions therein.

Vitality, the state of being vigorous and active, invokes notions of the seed that, with supporting humus, nutrients, sunlight and irrigation grow into a plant yielding the future seeds. Conceptual and technological inventions only become innovations when the conditions are right for lateral shifts and take-up in unanticipated contexts – windborne seeds blown to new gardens. Given the right conditions, inventions connect apparently separate ideas, materials or components and bring them into fresh concert – where they resonate with each other and things beyond themselves, forging the pathway to innovation: a vital difference to linear and predictable progression. This spread of resonances becomes a contagious 'newness' that conveys a living pulse. In these ways, vitality is always about collective or field conditions, pertaining to ecologies of material, social, economic and often imaginary interrelations (to name a few dimensions of the field) – the sustaining ingredients for innovation. Innovation in this light involves a sense of connection to a creative collective force beyond 'oneself' as creative individual. Such a vital force, evidenced in contributions across this issue, operates as the flip side to the various opposing forces of disconnection between creative individual and collective context such as depression, alienation and loneliness.

Joseph Paxton, The Crystal Palace, Hyde Park before being moved to Penge Common, London, 1851 (destroyed by fire 1936)
Paxton, who started his career as a gardener, became the architect of this, the world's largest ever glass building at the time. The project was only possible as an innovatory consequence of the British Industrial Revolution.

This amounts to thinking about innovation as a contagious, resonating shift in field conditions. Deeply and intrinsically situated, innovation brings with it the sense of vitality emerging out of the complexity of conditions through which it arose. Innovation is not just change arising through the potential of any such conditions, but a change in the conditions of the field such that new potential is felt – the sense that something more can now happen, but has not yet. As such, the kinds of practices that bring new potential to the surface are what we are most interested in here. Along these lines, one might define and recognise innovation from a qualitative perspective: as the feeling of emerging vitality, often appearing inexplicably resonant and expansively (even if intangibly) relevant.

Tools and technologies offer a considerable role in bringing new potential to the surface, playing a deeply significant role in driving innovation. Just as Vitruvius' *Ten Books on Architecture* were painstakingly scribed for his successors, the drivers of the Renaissance profited greatly from the inventors of the printing press. Today, both digital and biological technologies offer breathtakingly immense potential for designers who are being directed towards many different aspects and dimensions of architectural practice. Furthermore, our generation has the tools of immediate publication and effectively free dissemination through the Internet that, as a consequence, calls into question the status of hero individual in a generation that sees different priorities. There is a heightened sense of looking over each others' shoulders, of being part of a shared, distributed project, and less of a sense of being tied to convention – especially professional convention. This kind of cultural change, emerging in tandem with new technologies, also points to the fact that inventing tools and technologies is not the whole story of innovation, even if it is often mistaken as innovation itself. 'The Ethics of the Imperative' (pp 18–23) addresses how the way in which we approach the tools available to us becomes a key issue.

Our generation has the tools of immediate publication and effectively free dissemination through the Internet that, as a consequence, calls into question the status of hero individual in a generation that sees different priorities.

Norman Foster, Willis Faber & Dumas Headquarters, Ipswich, Suffolk, UK, 1975
below: Foster's Willis Faber & Dumas Headquarters turned many architectural norms on their heads as it rumbustiously made the planning envelope literally its own. Innovations were at many levels, including bringing the fully glazed walls out to the building's physical perimeter, the open planning and inclusion of a swimming pool within the interior, and the entire roof forming a garden. The invention of suspended glazing associated with the building makes it a landmark in 'high tech' architecture.

James Stirling, Faculty of History Library, Cambridge University, Cambridge, 1968
right: Regarded by many as the arrival of the atrium as a major architectural functional device to interiorise external space, the library, despite its many technical flaws, nevertheless had an innovation impact that still resonates around the world more than 40 years later.

Renzo Piano, Richard Rogers and Gianfranco Franchini, Centre Georges Pompidou, Paris, 1977
right: In the history of architectural innovation from this building onwards, building services could no longer be presumed to be inevitably tucked away out of sight, as here at the Centre Georges Pompidou they were celebrated for the first time. Other innovations included inventing structural technologies more familiar to bridge builders than to architects in order to create the magnificently generous column-free floor spaces within.

MOS (Michael Meredith and Hilary Sample), Pavillon Spéciale competition entry mock-ups, École Spéciale d'Architecture, New York studio, 2012
This kind of 'back-of-house' scene of material design experimentation in the studio is a crucial but rarely exposed aspect of architectural innovation. The often messy and provisional spaces and byproducts of the design research process are telling signs of the degree to which practices are willing to play, experiment and explore new potential.

Pia Ednie-Brown, *Plastic Futures*, State of Design Festival, Melbourne, 2009
The *Plastic Futures* installation and exhibition was a major outcome of a research workshop hosted by both RMIT's School of Architecture and Design and SymbioticA (University of Western Australia). This workshop negotiated a complex array of issues, with the core aim of exploring how speculative futures can be a potent agent for addressing the ethical implications of immanent vectors of innovation. The role and importance of playful, speculative architectural propositions is addressed in several essays in this issue of △.

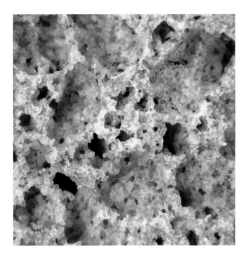

Ginger Krieg Dosier, VergeLabs/bioMASON, Bio-Manufactured Brick, 2012
Macro microscopy of biologically cemented UAE dune sand grains with air entrainment. As discussed in the essay on pp 84-91 of this issue, this technique for the biomanufacture of bricks has been explored by Greg Dosier in such a way that new interactions between diverse and distinct systems have been created.

In all these ways, innovation is not just a simple matter of newness. Ideas are constantly rising to the surface of cultural attention, submerging into relative obscurity after a period of development, to then reappear decades or even centuries later when conditions render them relevant once again, offering new potential to connect into a field of activity and develop. When something becomes new again, such as when the pointed arch of 19th-century Gothic Revival once again countered the inherent inefficiency of the revived classical rounded arch, it resonates not only with the conditions of the present moment, but also affords a fresh patina enriched through time. Even when reappearing in the guise of the new, the echoes of history – such as Le Corbusier's monastic sensibilities at La Tourette (1956–60) – are nevertheless implicitly embedded, deepening the power of innovation through the whispers of cultural memory. Innovation is the era-dependent, situated act of 'making a difference'. Innovation is always an event.

With this in mind, one must not forget that this publication and its take on the subject occur in a particular moment in time. Innovation, after all, is not the same thing in every moment in time or across all spaces. The urge to examine innovation more closely – and in relation to architecture in particular – is inflected by the broadly

Oron Catts and Ionat Zurr, *Victimless Leather: A Prototype of Stitch-less Jacket grown in a Technoscientific 'Body'*, Tissue Culture & Art Project, SymbioticA, School of Anatomy, Physiology and Human Biology, University of Western Australia, 2012
The artists use a range of media including a custom-made perfusion pump, biodegradable polymer, nutrient media and living cells. This project is a good example of the role and power of vitalist bioart in innovation ecologies (see pp 68–9 and p 91 of this issue). The claim for a 'victimless' product is intended as a provocation by the artists, who are attuned to the often hidden ethical problematics of biotechnologies.

The ways in which living creatures choose, adapt and construct their habitats becomes a potent evolutionary agent, introducing feedback into the evolutionary dynamic.

New Territories/R&Sie(n), Concrete bio-polymer secretions/extrusions/toolings/ weaving bio-concrete, 2010
Development of a secretion material whose viscosity and adhesiveness is compatible with the machinist protocol, using materials and procedures similar to the contour-crafting system developed with Behrokh Khoshnevis's laboratory at the University of Southern California for the 'I've heard about' project (FEIDAD award, 2005–6). This is an 'agricultural product', and does not use any fossil fuels, employing instead bio-resins as materials low in CO_2 emissions. The work of R&Sie(n) has been remarkable for the range of material and procedural experimentation they have undertaken in developing a diverse array of projects.

Could a new innovation imperative in fact be deemed to be key to architecture's survival as a practice?

Cloud 9 Architects (Enric Ruiz Geli), Media Tic, Barcelona, 2010
Innovation in construction, structure and service design (environmental responsiveness) ensured that this multipurpose office and exhibition building was not only constructed at a relatively low cost, but the innovations led to some startlingly original design features.

defining conditions of rapid change we find ourselves in. In conditions of low economic growth and a shaken faith in the notion that capitalism is a self-correcting system, there is a turbulent slowness in which innovation shows itself to be far more complex than a problem of confidently making new things, and generating more profit. Like those dreams when you can only run from danger in slow motion, or when you fall and a thickness of perception makes time expand inside the event, cultural innovation seems both pressing as a need and difficult to gel. While qualitative and social issues seem to be gaining more attention, and new models of political action such as the Occupy Movement are emerging and developing, there is a sense of being caught in a paradigm shift that we are – as yet – unable to clearly articulate. When it comes to the question of what to do next, what is required, what might help us with the challenges we face, nothing from the past or the recent present seems adequate: we cannot simply implement change from above, nor viably cast the future into the winds of a bottom-up emergence predicated on self-organising systems.

Linked tightly to spatio-temporal conditions, innovation is thereby always environmental. In his book *Where Good Ideas Come From: The Natural History of Innovation* (2010),[2] Steven Johnson emphasises the influence of environments on innovation arguing, for instance, that 'the physical architecture of our work environments can have a transformative effect on the quality of our ideas'.[3] In other words, architecture is not simply an outcome or an expression of our good ideas; it turns back and plays a part in constructing them. Along a related vein, John Odling-Smee, Kevin Laland and Marcus Feldman's book *Niche Construction* (2003)[4] presents a case for environments as an under-considered factor in evolutionary theory. As evolutionary biologists they argue that the ways in which living creatures choose, adapt and construct their habitats becomes a potent evolutionary agent, introducing feedback into the evolutionary dynamic. Again, constructed environments do not just evolve as part of 'natural' or cultural evolution; they play a hand in that evolution. As such, the influence of architecture on innovation ecologies should not be underestimated, and in better understanding the particularities of innovation in the realm of architectural production – a major task of this △ title – this becomes important well beyond the architectural discipline itself.

As such, approaching the topic of innovation in today's climate has also involved a search for how we might rethink and revitalise innovation within architectural practice – and how innovation itself might be innovated. As architectural practice is intrinsically tied to the construction of environments of so many different kinds, as the diversity of contributors here indicate, it has a particularly critical role to play in the evolutionary dynamic, especially as we hurtle towards environmental, civic and social challenges of unknown dimensions. Innovators today face complexities that cannot be addressed with the same level of confidence as the fathers of the first Congrès internationaux d'architecture moderne (CIAM) might have managed in 1928. Towards that end, the discursive stories we construct about innovation by architects should focus neither hermetically inwards (to architecture about architecture) nor forgetfully outwards to external concerns that ignore architectural practice and the vitality that architects can bring to teams addressing complex issues. Rather, we might productively aim our attention towards understanding how architectural practices might insinuate themselves more effectively within broader entanglements, and vice versa. We might also profitably focus on how architectural assemblages impact upon cultural activity seen through a lens that employs a more open, in-process, qualitative definition of architectural innovation than we are used to applying, which is what this issue of △ sets out to do.

Here we aim to take a bold step in that direction. This △ should be read as one particular take on innovation aimed at the contemporary state of affairs in which what properly constitutes the practice of architecture has become an increasingly complex question. What is most important in writing and developing the account we have built up here is that something new and worthwhile is being explored and drawn out: a deeper appreciation for what innovation might and could mean for architecture and other aesthetically defined, environmentally situated practices. Here we sample practices with wider, looser but more lively definitions of architectural innovation, united by their vital differences, as the contents of this issue attest. Could a new innovation imperative in fact be deemed to be key to architecture's survival as a practice? As designers we need to become ever more savvy and purposeful in the application of ideas and technologies, demonstrating that they can produce spaces that go beyond the mere baseline requirements of highly repetitive, economical, rolled-out units. As the scope and opportunities of virtual, speculative and curatorial activities take hold of the collective imagination, we may need to question the presumption that physical space has to be an intrinsic part of our practice. Despite the continuum that is the cyclical nature of history, plus ça change it is not, and we do not expect to return to 'business as usual'. △

Notes
1. Mark Wigley, 'Network Fever', *Grey Room 04*, MIT Press (Cambridge, MA), 2001, p 114.
2. Steven Johnson, *Where Good Ideas Come From: The Natural History of Innovation*, Riverhead Books (New York), 2010.
3. Ibid, p 62.
4. John Odling-Smee, Kevin Laland and Marcus Feldman, *Niche Construction: The Neglected Process in Evolution*, Princeton University Press (Princeton, NJ), 2003.

Pia Ednie-Brown

THE ETHICS OF THE IMPERATIVE

The bald desire to innovate is not sufficient in itself. To go beyond mere technical invention and make a positive difference, innovation requires an engagement with overall ethical intent. Here, Guest-Editor **Pia Ednie-Brown** espouses a design ethos that values an open-ended approach to architectural innovation. She illustrates the ethical impact of implementing new technologies with two opposing paradigms – one dark and one affirmative – as exemplified by two classic films from 1968: *2001: A Space Odyssey* and *Barbarella*.

Film still from *Barbarella*, Roger Vadim, 1968
Entrapped in the 'excessive machine', Durand Durand tries to
kill Barbarella. Her subsequent triumph over the killing machine
involves a mode of virtuosity that becomes a reference point
across many articles in this issue, as an exemplary model for
approaching the innovation imperative.

Film still from *2001: A Space Odyssey*, Stanley Kubrick, 1968
In the opening sequences of Kubrick's film, set in the prehistoric Pleistocene era, we are presented with the paradigmatic 'Ah-ha' moment of invention, where the ape-man realises the potential of a bone as a tool. This invention leads to innovation, as the relations conditioning the Pleistocene environment alter, with new kinds of predation and defence emerging, changing relationships between different organisms, and between primates and objects, for instance. As discussed here, however, this is indicative of an instrumental understanding of invention, and suggestive of the darker side of innovation and its imperatives.

In 1968, Stanley Kubrick unleashed his film *2001: A Space Odyssey*, from a screenplay co-written with Arthur C Clarke. While set in the (then) future, the film begins with the prehistoric, where a group of primates are woken at dawn by an operatically singing, smooth black obelisk: an alien intelligence. Soon after, one of these apes – an alpha-male called Moon-Watcher in Clarke's accompanying novel – plays with skeletal remains scattered across a dry landscape. The potential of these bones as a tool gradually dawns on him, and he eventually works out that he could smash a skull into spectacular smithereens. This leads to a scene in which Moon-Watcher bludgeons another from a competing tribe to death in a territorial dispute over a watering hole.

The relations constituting this Pleistocene landscape are forever altered: animals become food rather than simply competitors for resources, predators can be fought in new ways, a new kind of warfare between apes comes into being, and objects such as bones attain a new status altogether. In this way, the invention of a tool becomes innovation. Memorably, Moon-Watcher throws the bone into the air in a triumphant and exuberantly expressed 'Ah-ha!' moment. The camera follows the upward tumbling motion of the bone in slow motion, until a montage cut transforms the bone into a spacecraft floating in the black of space. Traversing millions of years in a single cut, we jump from a proto-human instance of innovation – transforming the field of play – to the future unfolding of that field.

What might this story tell us about how we conceptualise the roots of the innovation imperative? Kubrick's *2001* might be taken as a kind of solemn reminder that there can be a darker side of innovation; that a competitive, destructive drive underwrites the imperative, quietly inflecting (or infecting?) the field of activity in which it operates.

This dark portrayal of the innovation imperative can be juxtaposed with another film from 1968. *Barbarella* (directed by Roger Vadim) offers a very different story about innovation. In one of the more memorable scenes of the film, the figure of evil, Durand Durand, tries to kill Barbarella with an 'excessive machine': a large rubber-and-plastic piano-meets-bed-like device that induces such heights of ecstasy in women that it kills them.

An analogy between the bone in *2001* and the excessive machine as killing tools is irresistible here. Durand Durand becomes the virtuoso of death as he plays a musical score to drive the machine, telling Barbarella that when he reaches the crescendo she will die a swift and sweet death. But not only does she survive it; it does not survive her. Her extended orgasm overcomes the machine, which smokes and finally bursts into flames. As Reyner Banham wrote in 'Triumph of Software', a laudatory 1968 review of the film, 'the insatiability of her flesh burns its wiring and blows its circuits'.[1]

The most instructive thing about this counter-example lies in a shift of the status of the tool. As Durand Durand wields his

Alisa Andrasek and Jose Sanchez, *BLOOM*, Victoria Park and Trafalgar Square, London, 2012
This interactive system was conceived as an urban game, a distributed social toy and collective 'gardening' experience that seeks the engagement of people in order to construct fuzzy bloom formations throughout the city. Initial series of ground configurations are laid out to provoke and engage the public. The pink, injection-moulded plastic *BLOOM* cell is 100 per cent recyclable, with the work overall being considered as a mode of assembly, disassembly and reusability.

evolved, musical bone-weapon, played with the intention of doing her over, Barbarella invents a new kind of instrument that is not so much a device per se, but a kind of virtuosity that involves riding a fine line of both 'doing' and 'being done'. She does not try to control the killing machine, but neither does she become submissive. As the machine affects her, she moves with it, literally giving back that which is being performed upon her, producing an internal feedback loop and transforming the event from the inside. Barbarella had the power to both affect and be affected, such that her adversary, a machine made only to work in one direction, was overpowered by its own aim. Software, introducing feedback and nonlinearity into the system, triumphs over unidirectional hardware.

What is important about the bone, then, is not just what it is (because it certainly has the potential to be used for many things, not just kill), but what drives its use (the imperative that moves things along). In the aggressively instrumental stance, we know what the desired outcome is before it is achieved (ie, kill) – it is really just a matter of getting it done. Barbarella, on the other hand, did not know where this would lead, expressing some surprise and regret over the now flaming and spluttering machine-cum-lover. What mattered was that she operated precisely on the line of simultaneously affecting and being affected – not as two separate acts, but as part of the one act of engagement. The excessive machine scene is one of many instances

across the broader narrative trajectory of the film, where Barbarella gradually increases her capacity to move, quite literally and physically, into the tissue of circumstances in allowing new forms of the world to emerge – or in other words, to innovate.

It would be a mistake to think that the instrumental approach is not without an appreciation of process, or of taking pleasure in the unfolding of relations; Durand Durand delighted in killing through pleasure, just as the ape might have gained pleasure in the act of bludgeoning. But when the predetermined goal is made to happen externally, rather than allowed to emerge through an intricate negotiation from within the situation, there is less room for more implicit or quietly lingering potential to surface and become explicit. If we expand the idea of the machine to the cultural, economic and material systems we inhabit – and the 'excessive machine' seems an apt analogue for the capitalist machine – *Barbarella* becomes a parable for the kind of virtuosity one might aim to develop in seeking an ethical approach to the imperative for innovation.

In terms of design practices, the kind of approach being pointed to here by invoking Barbarella finds one trajectory in computational design and material form finding, examples of which can be found in collections such as Mark Fornes' curated exhibition and website, 'Scripted by Purpose' (2007),[2] in Mark Burry's book *Scripting Cultures* (2011),[3] Gail Peter Borden and Michael Meredith's *Matter: Material Processes*

Eva Franch i Gilabert, Strategies for Public Occupation, Storefront for Art and Architecture, New York, 2011
Storefront for Art and Architecture, directed by Eva Franch i Gilabert, set up a series of events in direct response to the Occupy Movement, a movement that arose internationally against social and economic inequality. In October 2011, Storefront put out a call for submissions for projects and strategies that proposed new, creative and productive approaches to spatial occupation, for public demonstrations and actions in cities throughout the world in order to enable communication and exchange between the civil society and the structures of economic and political power. This led to an exhibition and a seven-day programme of talks, workshops and events through which to generate ideas and discuss the current state of affairs in relation to the Occupy Movement around the world.

in Architectural Production (2012),[4] and the recent △ *Material Computation* (2012), guest edited by Achim Menges.[5] Across these collections, one can see a clear shift away from the kinds of authorial mythologies that locate creative 'genius' entirely within the architect. At their best, these design approaches involve working with materials (physical, digitally described and/or social and conceptual systems and substances) in a way that guides the formation of a project in desired directions while negotiating or working with the tendencies, characteristics and 'wilfulness' of that material.

In a recent essay, computational design architect Roland Snooks, of kokkugia, distinguishes between working with generative algorithms – in ways that accept a messy volatility – and 'form finding', which he sees as risk averse and equilibrium seeking.[6] The more open volatility he advocates has an affinity with the design ethos being advocated here, and similar traits are fairly emphatically expressed through the work of other digital design practices. However, digital computation is not a prerequisite for related approaches. The diverse cast and the very different practices in this issue aim to gather a broad, expanded sense of the value of open-ended approaches for architectural innovation, and ways in which working across many media and dimensions might be important. One could line up the practices and projects of, for example,

architects Alisa Andrasek, Eva Franch i Gilabert and Veronika Valk and discern a productive through-line or affinity in their desire to enable or initiate participation, to expand their engagement beyond architects or conventional architectural media, and to encourage collectively acquired value – each through extraordinarily different means, modes and media. Moving transversally across engagements with socio-cultural events, digital and biological media, models of community and urbanism, and imagined, speculative propositions, *The Innovation Imperative* explores the importance and role of working in multiple modes and media – but also the importance of seeking affinities beyond obvious clusterings or architectural 'styles' in gathering a sense of what is emerging across the bigger field of architectural exploration.

It is worth noting here that the kind of virtuosity this implies, particularly when involving digital computation, is too often mistaken as the abdication of intent, or the 'giving over' of authorship. This strangely persistent critique is not a logical necessity, and quite ironically operates in sympathy with the problematic notion of the 'creative genius', who uncompromisingly implements his or her visionary design ideas. The affinity between these positions – 'hands off' self-organisation and the stamp of individual genius – can also be found in the notion that economic systems are entirely self-correcting. Commonly wielded as a neo-liberal weapon, this notion is used to argue that care and responsibility for

Veronika Valk, *Swinging In The Light*, Tallinn Festival of Light, Tallinn, Estonia, 2006
This mobile hotel offers an open invitation to spend time outdoors despite the somewhat extreme Estonian wintertime conditions, where temperatures can fall to −35°C (−31°F). At night, these super-sized, insulated white hammocks are illuminated and heated further by directional infrared lamps.

collective interest can be abdicated (because the self-correcting system takes care of that), giving the self-interested individual the right to care exclusively for that self-interest (and his or her uncompromising vision). But the more realistic and ethical alternative is something more co-defining: individuals who 'stand out' become important instigators, being affected, inflected and moved by collective entanglements while affecting the tangle in turn. To some degree the individual and the collective are always in tension, together generating intention. Along these lines, intentionality in design cannot be absolved, but rather relocated. Rather than being inside the individual, intention is generated in an outside – as part of the tensions between collective and individual insight and concern.

If we are feeling the imperative to innovate, we need to grapple with intention in order to navigate the ethics of our actions. The kind of virtuosity being referred to here, fleshed out via *Barbarella*, becomes a way to work with an intent to negotiate pressures from within situations and events, to navigate the concerns of others and the many material properties of the world without losing one's way: to find an ethics for approaching the imperative for architectural innovation. However, we can only get so far towards an understanding of what any of this means for architecture through *Barbarella*. Across this issue of △ are a series of more targeted architectural stories through which to speak of related acts within the spectrum of individual and collective virtuosity. △

The diverse cast and the very different practices in this issue aim to gather a broad, expanded sense of the value of open-ended approaches for architectural innovation, and ways in which working across many media and dimensions might be important.

Notes
1. Reyner Banham, 'The Triumph of Software', *New Society*, Vol 12, No 318, 31 October 1968, pp 629–30.
2. 'Scripted by Purpose' exhibition and website, curated by Marc Fornes, Philadelphia, September 2007: http://scriptedbypurpose. wordpress.com/.
3. Mark Burry, *Scripting Cultures: Architectural Design and Programming*, John Wiley & Sons (Chichester), 2011.
4. Gail Peter Borden and Michael Meredith (eds), *Matter: Material Processes in Architectural Production*, Routledge (London and New York), 2012.
5. Achim Menges (ed), △ *Material Computation: Higher Integration in Morphogenetic Design*, March/April (no 2), 2012.
6. Roland Snooks, 'Volatile Formation', *Log* 25, Summer 2012, pp 55–62.

Mark Burry

DESIGN AND SOCIETY

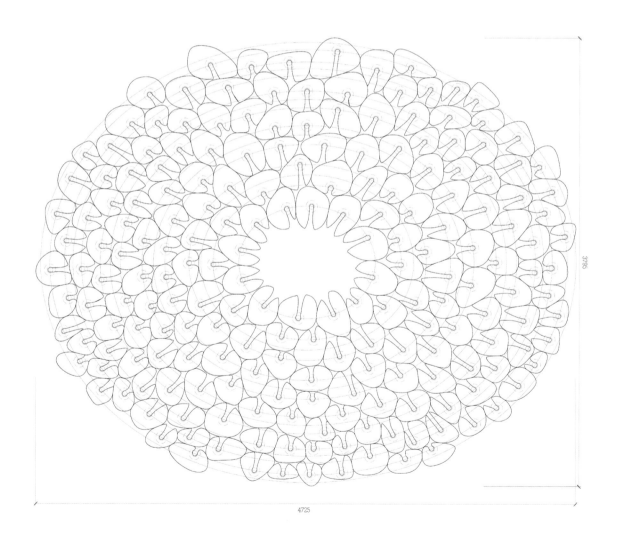

3795

4725

INNOVATION THROUGH APPROPRIATION AND ADAPTATION

'To strive for a culture framed on great design is itself a fundamental innovation imperative.' Here, Guest-Editor **Mark Burry** poses the difficult question of how innovation might be achieved at a wider cultural level. How can society effectively seek to demand great design with confidence and authority? Burry looks specifically at the role of the design commissioner and the challenge of creating an overarching design system, as exemplified by the figure of Frank Pick, who in the first half of the 20th century steered London Underground's design identity, developing its enduring, highly distinctive graphics and architecture.

Heatherwick Studio, Olympic Cauldron, London, 2012

In order to take stock of the current innovation imperative, we need to understand what is different this time around. Innovation has routinely become part of governmental rhetoric and, occasionally, even the Zeitgeist, but governments seldom proselytise a lead role for design. At times the rhetoric is quite powerful, as in the former prime minister of Great Britain Harold Wilson's 1963 oft-quoted exhortation for the emerging era to be framed by the 'white heat' of technology – a technological innovation imperative.[1]

'Innovation': such an important word and often so trivially applied. Its casual synonymy to design through loose association risks a reduction in its meaning. Recent politicisation of innovation places yet more obstacles to non-designers' comprehension of 'design', both verb and noun. An easy conjunction such as 'innovative design', for instance, if not an actual tautology, at least begs the question of what non-innovative design might be, and who is doing it. Equally, the differences between 'original', 'novel', 'inventive' and 'innovative' are blurred through lazy language use to the extent that should the general populace believe in unoriginal, non-novel, uninventive and non-innovative design, design risks being ascribed with an ill-founded credibility: design used as a label or brand.

This short essay considers the role of the design commissioner and argues that individual design brilliance is usually not enough to both influence and educate the end user. Frank Pick (1878–1941) is identified as a model for instituting an enlightened and effective approach to ensure design excellence wherever possible while endorsing the efforts of the creative individual.

A Quaker from the north of England, Pick was a talented manager and not a creative: a civil servant to the core yet chief protagonist for the establishment in 1915 of the Design and Industries Association (DIA) that led to some of the best years of British design innovation extending through to the Second World War and beyond. Pick rapidly rose through the ranks of the Underground Electric Railways Company of London, which he had joined in 1906, and when it became the London Passenger Transport Board in 1933 he was CEO and Vice-Chairman, positions he retained until 1940. His career was a testament of both a singular drive and clarity of vision.

Through design, designers expect to improve on an existing situation, product, service or system, and as such this can be considered a utopian view.[2] To add to a sense of urgency we can use the imperative voice; designers therefore *must* ensure that their activities are novel, inventive and innovative by definition, for without such essential ingredients 'design' is little more than a pattern, model, exemplar, facsimile, copy, mimesis or version. When design commissioners, customers, critics and end users *demand* design innovation to be more than just a brand or marque, design is elevated to being a cultural imperative that makes such a difference to society. What is the connection between the design innovator and the design commissioner in this regard – how well do we understand the connection, and who brokers it? There is indeed a vital connection between the two, but regrettably they are fused together far too seldom for reasons that are difficult to elicit.

Culture framed around the benefits of good design offers greater social capital than that framed on the business case supported by designers pulling together and awarding prizes to each other: good design has substance, great design has substance and long-lasting impact. To strive for a culture framed on great design is itself a fundamental innovation imperative, one predicated on innovation *across* designers as well as *within* a design discipline. Society must therefore demand great design with confidence and authority and, judging how few countries can demonstrate a design culture embedded intrinsically within their general populace, there is obviously a significant challenge for us all.

To succeed, a clarity of purpose – intentionality – is required across all design disciplines, regardless of the type of design approach adopted in order to separate 'great' design from merely the 'good'. Appropriations and adaptations through taking design approaches out of their original context and experimentally speculating greatly assist the ability to innovate with lasting impact. The terms of reference for attaining a higher level of commitment to design excellence, in the public sphere at least, must include the challenge of creating a design *system* rather than on collections of designed *objects* as the essential outcomes. By this route we can move on to common higher ground and consider design commissioners (or patrons) as exponents of innovation-through-appropriation as much as the designers. In doing so, innovation-through-appropriation's alter ego, innovation-through-misappropriation, can be deemed as not relevant; a last refuge for the designer dilettante unencumbered by the necessary gifts with which to ideate, conceive or create, however naughty, postmodern, democratic and exciting this construction of alternative design might be. Enfranchising the dilettante is unlikely to lead to the design-conscious society that Frank Pick felt inspired to create, so this essay is about harnessing the best to make the most positive difference to society through design.

Frank Pick and the Design and Industries Association (DIA)

There is irony in designers' essential (and laudable) disinclination to conform, thereby compounding the consumers' and end users' sense of a lack of coherence from their viewpoint. This mismatch results partially in design being seen as lacking economic significance in many regions of the world, and certainly not being crucial culturally.

There is an implicit equation where 'good design = improved quality', acting as a core ingredient of effective decision-making that draws upon a longer-term value proposition. Occasionally good design and good value intersect, buoyed by the right marketing approach and a cost differential from lesser goods and services that is not too exaggerated. External factors can intervene negatively in terms of local economy where a public, ordinarily purblind to the value of design, nevertheless discerns a product being superior for other, more mundane attributes such as simply functioning better. Voting through their purchasing habits, even design Philistines can inadvertently up the status of design. An example of this was the surge in sales of teapots and other utilitarian manufactured goods imported to the UK from Germany in the decade before the First World War. The output from local industry was seen as being inferior in quality, but the move away from British-made goods was also a secondary reaction to the pomposity of Victorian

To any who wonder how the apparent timelessness of design classics from that age came to be, the credit goes entirely to Frank Pick and the DIA, and not least to the designers they spotted and commissioned.

design exacerbated by the Edwardian taste for the florid and exaggerated that followed.

There is an irony here. While British consumers were increasingly turning away from locally designed and manufactured goods, in his native Germany Hermann Muthesius (1861–1927) was extolling the virtues of *Das englische Haus*.[3] For the Westminster parliamentarians with the responsibility for boosting prosperity for the local manufacturers, the effect of the establishment of the Deutscher Werkbund (German Work Federation) in 1907 was a powerful stimulant for them to do something similar in the UK, leading to the establishment of the Design and Industries Association (DIA) in Great Britain eight years later. How dramatically they managed to reverse the declining interest in British-manufactured goods is underplayed by the national psyche of the time, there being no national design press through which to extol the adding of value that designers could bring. The chief protagonists for a design-led recovery to an otherwise moribund sector, such as Frank Pick, were neither designers themselves nor especially egotistical in their endeavours as public patrons of design, not to suggest otherwise that effectiveness and ego necessarily have to go hand in hand.

To any who wonder how the apparent timelessness of design classics from that age came to be, the credit goes entirely to Frank Pick and the DIA, and not least to the designers they spotted and commissioned. Charles Holden (1875–1960) was the principal architect for the growing metropolitan railway system during Pick's years, and a fellow northerner (and Quaker too). The quietly authoritative pared-back classicism of Holden's tube stations on the southern (Morden) extension to the Northern line, and his very English contribution to the International Style through the stations he designed later for the eastward extension to the Central line, came about entirely as a result of Pick's perspicacious and careful selection of just who would design the public face of a major expansion to London's transport infrastructure that was so critical for the successful development of the suburbs.

Paul Nash, British Industries Fair poster, 1935
Artist, designer and writer Paul Nash was a pioneer of Modernism in Britain, introducing elements of Surrealism and abstraction to the English landscape painting tradition. As Pick commissioned more and more leading artists to design posters for the Underground, the gap between avant-garde art and commercial graphic design began to close.

Douglas MacPherson, Piccadilly Circus Station, stomach diagram, 1928
Douglas Macpherson, another contemporary artist/illustrator commissioned by Pick, designed posters for the Underground from 1927 to 1933. This diagram illustrates Charles Holden's desire to repeat the aboveground circus with his belowground ticketing hall. The hall connects to a succession of escalators, staircases, tunnels and links to platforms; its construction was a highly regarded engineering feat at the time.

Edward Johnston, Johnston Sans Serif font, 1916
Frank Pick commissioned Edward Johnston to design a typeface that could be clearly read on all of the Underground Group's signage. After nearly three years in production, Johnston delivered a classic in modern lettering. Slightly reworked over the years, the Johnston typeface is still in use by Transport for London today.

Edward McKnight Kauffer, The Flea at the Natural History Museum, 1926
A prolific and influential graphic designer, Edward McKnight Kauffer expressed Cubism, Futurism and Surrealism in the 140 posters he designed for the Underground.

Charles Holden/Adams, Holden & Pearson Architects, 55 Broadway, Westminster, London, 1929
top: Commissioned by Pick to design the new Underground headquarters, Holden made a daring architectural statement by assuming the cruciform plan as a way of dealing with the irregular-shaped site. Holden commissioned artists Jacob Epstein, AH Gerrard, Eric Gill, Allan Wyon, Eric Aumonier, Samuel Rabinovitch and Henry Moore to carve figurative reliefs on the facade. The overt 'Modernism' and explicit nudity of some of the sculptures generated negative press and community uproar when the building opened.

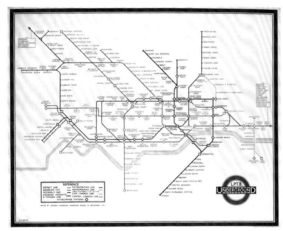

FH Stingemore, Pocket Underground Map, 1931
centre: Deemed too complicated, this Underground map design immediately predates the classic redesign by Harry Beck that is still in use today

Harry C Beck, London Underground Map, 1933
bottom: An uncommissioned idea from a young engineering draughtsperson, Harry Beck, who redesigned the Underground map as a simple diagram, recognising that the perspective of the belowground traveller was not their relative location above ground, but the connections between 'lines', and not the lines themselves.

Pick exerted the same philosophy in all aspects for what is now the London Underground and its related aboveground buildings, infrastructure and service design. This is evidenced by his selection of graphic designer Edward Johnston (1872–1944), whom he commissioned in 1913. Aided by artist Eric Gill, Johnston gave us the Johnston Sans Serif font, which seems as fresh today as when it first emerged in 1916, almost a century ago. Pick ensured that poster sizes were standardised so as to be incorporated architecturally in the new stations and not displayed ad hoc. In the same spirit he identified emerging artists such as Paul Nash (1889–1946) and graphic designers such as Edward McKnight Kauffer (1890–1954) to design the posters and, controversially, sculptors such as Jacob Epstein (1880–1959) to work with Holden on the more substantial building commissions, including 55 Broadway, the transport company's headquarter offices occupying a whole block with its distinctive cruciform plan.

Innovation Through Design

The innovation of a topologically consistent yet topographically relaxed mapping of the Underground network, the first-edition 'tube map' by Harry Beck (1902–74), released publicly after development in 1933, hardly needs reference here, as belatedly his contribution has been justly recognised, though apparently not during his lifetime.[4] An updated version of Beck's map, originally commissioned by Pick in 1931, is still extant 80 years later. It is favoured not simply because it is quirkily effective, but because it also looks authoritative and user-friendly: it exudes design quality. Over the decades it has achieved an iconic status that matches its practicality and is a highly credible example of innovation through appropriation and adaptation. Beck trained as a draughtsman and recognised that the perspective of the belowground traveller was not their geographical location above ground, but their focus on the connections between 'lines': not the lines themselves. It seems that Beck realised that the belowground voyager, having switched off their aboveground cognitive faculties, was not substituting these with their imagination, as a child might. It has been suggested that Beck was influenced by electronic circuit-board diagrams, which seems likely given that such a creative leap from a geographically rich context aboveground to the subterranean is what designers do with such effect: an apparently effortless shift between contexts.[5] In terms of impact, Beck's design innovation is at the highest level, as so many cities around the world have adopted his model.

Of all the outcomes from the period that have withstood the test of time, it is Beck's map that makes the point about impactful design most effectively. It is a designed *object* that came about within a design *system* set up specifically not to honour designers necessarily (or in Beck's case not at all), but to provide the public with something that 'just works' (not to coin a phrase) and a design that was at the same time intellectually edifying.

In terms of the various consequential shifts within the design Zeitgeist of the time, Nikolaus Pevsner (1902–83) covers this territory well in his time-honoured *Pioneers of the Modern Movement* (1936), but places relatively little emphasis on how the country's political and industrial leadership dealt with the growing economic inferiority in the manufacturing sector.[6] Perhaps it was the timing of the first edition in 1936, so soon after Pevsner had arrived in England as a refugee from Nazi

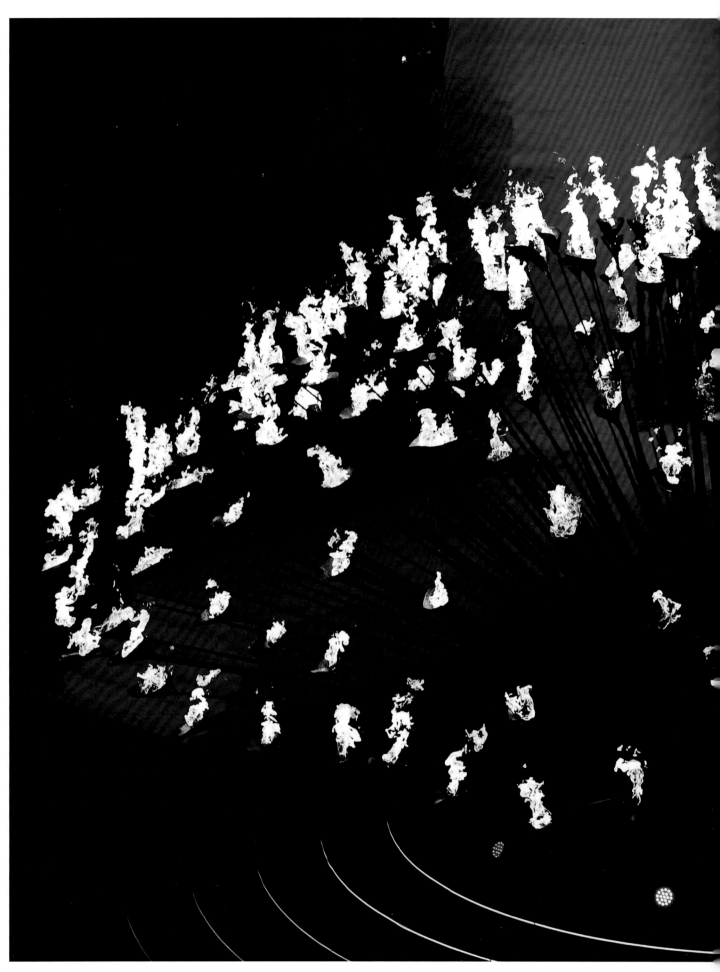

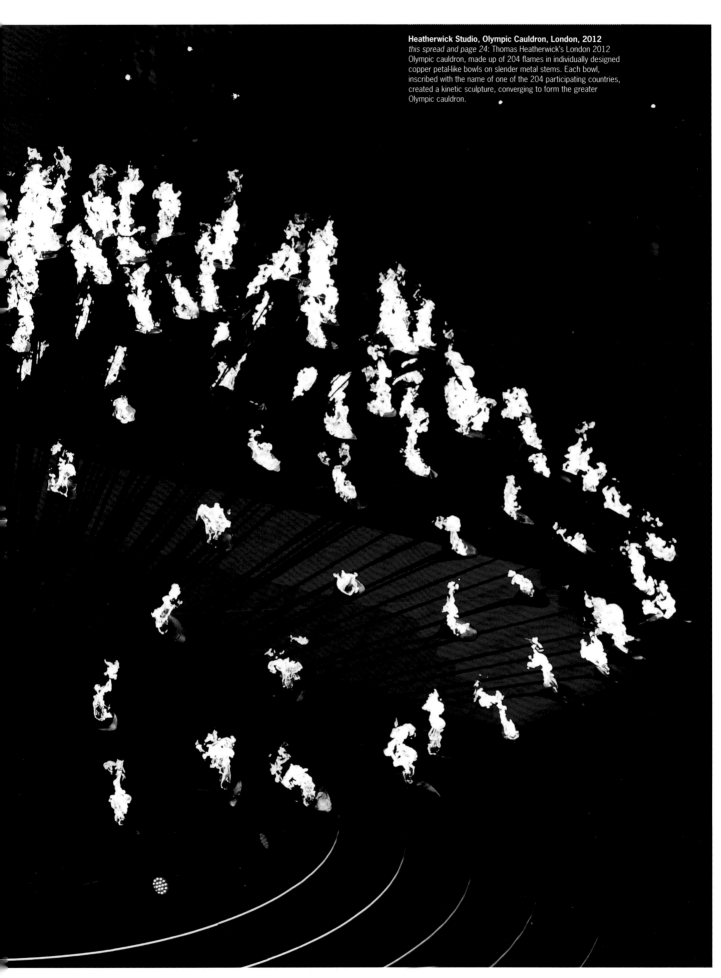

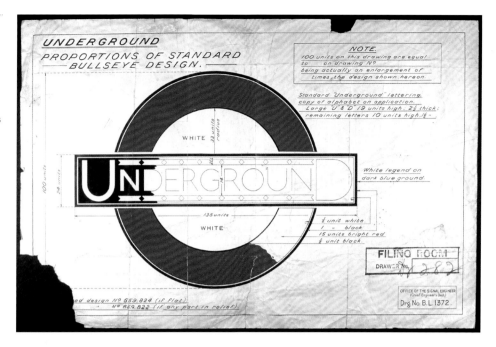

Original drawing of the registered design version of the Johnston roundel, 1925
In 1913, Frank Pick commissioned Edward Johnston to incorporate his new typeface with the existing station signage: a solid red disc and horizontal blue bar. Through his reworking of the red disc into a circle and the use of his new logotype, the Underground roundel was born, and remains the logo for London's transport system to this day.

As designers we need to help effect the major innovation imperative of enlightened public and private design 'patronage', but this requires working collectively beyond our professional disciplines in order to help create such a framework.

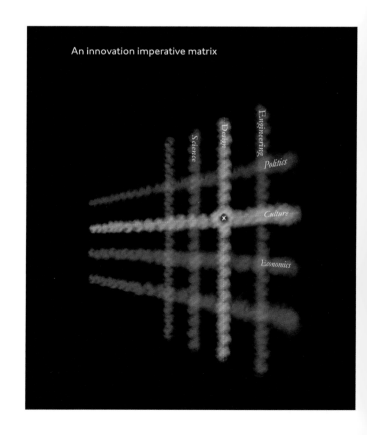

Mark Burry, Innovation Blur, 2012
The white heat of design innovation centred at the intersections of myriad social contexts and streams of expertise. In this diagram the white hotspot is exemplified when Frank Pick's design imperative is intersected with the selection and commission of other brilliant designers of his time.

Germany in 1933, that led to neither Pick nor Holden getting any mention in the book, and the DIA only the most cursory acknowledgement despite two decades of conspicuous activity from the Association.

This, the most cursory of accounts about one of the most effective design commissioning 'systems' of all time, cannot do it justice here. Naturally the situation was for more complex than it first might appear as the DIA coincided with the decades when Britain sought to converge 'art' fully with (industrial) 'design' to the extent that tertiary education in both fields merged.[7] The deliberate fusing of the fields of art and (industrial) design was argued philosophically and enacted practically until the 1950s when the two were deliberately decoupled and went along their different routes that they still follow today. Even Pick seemed to recant in this regard, and one senses he died quite a disappointed man despite all he achieved as a design commissioner and as the first chairman of the DIA.[8]

Lessons for Tomorrow

Pick's legacy is one of lateral diffusion of design excellence within society using a large assortment of exceptional designers drawn from a wide variety of design disciplines.[9] Many of the designs he commissioned, in some cases almost a century ago, live on, through surviving examples such as the Underground 'Roundel' identity, the Johnston typeface, the Beck map, the educational role of the poster extending well beyond public information and corporate branding and, not least, the architecture, much of it now listed. It is not just the design excellence, itself so 'fit for purpose' at the time, but the longevity of the design value that is being lauded here as a rich legacy extraordinary for the relative anonymity of the design commissioners.[10] Johnston's sans serif font is universally available, with many variants having emerged with the passage of time, and Beck's map remains a highly influential global model so many decades later.

Contemporary designers such as Jonathan Ive at Apple, the acknowledged maestro behind the company's range of tactile and intuitive user-friendly products, can joggle along fine within supportive corporate structures: the purpose, ultimately, is corporate profit through value adding by design. It might therefore seem hard to argue for any particular public good beyond the fact that every Apple computer purchased represents one less beige box and a community of happy design-educated consumers. Ive, however, acknowledges the influence that former maestros have had on his work, and it can be argued that individual designers will influence the next generation in ways that schools of design probably cannot achieve.[11] Beyond exceptional designers, we need public leaders who not only understand the social and cultural imperative of commissioning the best in design, but are also effective in getting it all to happen.

As designers we need to help effect the major innovation imperative of enlightened public and private design 'patronage', but this requires working collectively beyond our professional disciplines in order to help create such a framework. Unfortunately, in this respect, Pick seems to have been highly unusual: unique during his lifetime and relatively obscure following his death, and his like seems even further from view today.[12] Thus there is no obvious trajectory for designers to provide public design commissioners with the meta-design

understanding and ability required to integrate design within their undertakings instead of just seeking at best a distinctive 'designerly' overlay to those undertakings.[13]

Exceptional designers produce exceptional designs, but how might designers help create a system whereby excellence can be encouraged without subsuming individual brilliance into some anonymous collective? There is an abundance of opportunity here – transport systems, government departments, public institutions, major events to name a few, but sadly we suffer from almost the same degree of lost opportunity. At the time of writing, Thomas Heatherwick's London 2012 Olympic cauldron, made up of 204 flames in copper petal-like bowls – innovative at every level – makes this point most eloquently. Why is his contribution an exception to the event and not part of the 'white heat' of design that society so critically needs? ⌂

Notes

1. 'The Britain that is going to be forged in the white heat of this revolution will be no place for restrictive practices or for outdated methods on either side of industry.' Extract from Brian Walden, 'The White Heat of Wilson', http://news.bbc.co.uk/2/hi/uk_news/magazine/4865498.stm.
2. In the sense of Utopia as 'An impossibly ideal scheme, esp. for social improvement'. Utopia, n. Oxford English Dictionary, second edition, 1989; online version June 2012: http://www.oed.com/view/Entry/220784, accessed 18 April 2012. Earlier version first published in *New English Dictionary*, 1926.
3. Hermann Muthesius, *Das englische Haus* (*The English House*), Ernst Wasmuth (Berlin), 1904.
4. 'Beck received 5 guineas for the printing of the pocket map, 10 for the printing of the poster, and this is all he would ever be paid – the equivalent of about £400 in today's money.' Andrew Martin, *Underground, Overground: A Passenger's History of the Tube*, Profile Books (London), 2012, Kindle edition, location 2907.
5. Martin, op cit, Kindle edition, location 2903.
6. Nikolaus Pevsner, *Pioneers of the Modern Movement from William Morris to Walter Gropius*, Faber and Faber (London), 1936.
7. 'England, with the foundation of the D.I.A., was not early in taking up the programme developed by the Werkbund. Other Continental countries had followed Germany before the war: the Austrian Werkbund dates from 1910, the Swiss from 1913; and the Swedish Slöjdsforening was gradually reshaped into a Werkbund between 1910 and 1917.' Pevsner, op cit, Kindle edition, location 737.
8. The philosophy behind Pick et al, pitted as 'Medieval Modernists', is brilliantly unwrapped by Michael Saler in *The Avant-Garde in Interwar England: Medieval Modernism and the London Underground*, Oxford University Press (Oxford), 1999.
9. Aspects of Pick's vision live on within London Transport, such as the recent extension of the Jubilee line, but this is an 'architectural imperative', and not a holistic design imperative. See: www.tfl.gov.uk/corporate/modesoftransport/londonunderground/keyfacts/13172.aspx#page-link-architecture-on-the-jubilee-line, accessed 8 August 2012.
10. This was a guiding philosophy and slogan for the DIA.
11. Jonathan Ive and Apple have long acknowledged the influence of Dieter Rams and his ground-breaking design for Braun in Germany, starting in the 1950s. See: www.telegraph.co.uk/technology/apple/8555503/Dieter-Rams-Apple-has-achieved-something-I-never-did.html, accessed 8 August 2012.
12. 'There have been few studies of Pick. Christian Barman, who wrote a general biography, and Nikolaus Pevsner, who wrote the first (and still the best) extended essay on Pick as a patron of the arts, had the advantage of working with him, but they did not have access to the extensive archive on the Council for Art and Industry at the Public Record Office, which contains a great deal of illuminating material by and about Pick.' Saler, op cit, Kindle edition, location 3246.
13. It is not the intention to claim here that design and innovation are synonymous, but to observe that some innovation is more design driven than others, and we might agree that the ultimate measure of success is the degree of design impact and its longevity: design that lasts versus design as a fashion.

Pia Ednie-Brown

'Aesthetics/Anesthetics', Storefront
for Art and Architecture, New York,
2012
The Storefront space operates with an
unusual openness to the sidewalk.

INNOVATION AT THE STOREFRONT

An event and exhibition space opening on to the sidewalk
of New York City's SoHo, Storefront is dedicated to the
advancement of innovative positions in architecture and
design. It seeks 'to simultaneously shake and question the
current state of affairs'. Guest-Editor **Pia Ednie-Brown**
discusses with the Catalan architect, **Eva Franch i Gilabert**,
her role as Director of Storefront, and specifically how
she has promoted active, generative engagement through
humour, disruption and innovation.

Eva Franch i Gilabert, *Composite figure,* **2003–10**
Franch's interest in both excess and the ecological is evident in the
image used to portray the multifaceted nature of her architectural
practice OOAA (office of architectural affairs).

THE PRACTICE OF EVA FRANCH i GILABERT

Founded in 1982, Storefront for Art and Architecture in New York City has a 30-year history of providing an alternative platform for supporting new ideas in architecture and design. Storefront's narrow triangular building, redesigned by Steven Holl and Vito Acconci in 1993, literally unfolds its facade on to the street, becoming something between a gallery/event space and an extension of the footpath. Storefront's programme has always aligned itself with the unconventional and the experimental, and with the productively blurred zones between art and architecture. An explicit mandate is to support the innovative in ways that other institutions do not or cannot provide. As a swelling of the sidewalk, Storefront can be seen as a uniquely important architectural budding of the innovation imperative.

In 2010, the Catalan architect Eva Franch i Gilabert became the new director of Storefront. She previously directed the Masters Thesis studio at Rice University and her own solo practice, OOAA (office of architectural affairs). Her interest in 'ecologies of excess', demonstrated in her *D* article of that name in 2010,[1] reveals her emphasis upon speculative, experimental, broadly defined notions of ecologies as a way into architectural thought and action. Referring back to 'The Ethics of the Imperative' article on pp 18–23 of this issue, with Franch directing this eventful swelling of the sidewalk, Storefront could be seen as a truly architectural 'excessive machine', unfolding a related ethics of the imperative.

Franch's approach to directing Storefront for Art and Architecture involves inhabiting a tensile balance between individual action and collective engagement, offering an emphatic demonstration of a practice which values and enacts attention to both simultaneously. She designs events for Storefront that try 'to articulate obsessions into positions, to construct arguments and create conversations that bring people – who might perhaps be too focused within themselves – into a larger collective, or into a larger understanding of their work … and with that, figure out what they carry as individuals to contribute into the larger whole of society in order to go beyond what we already know'.[2] Her directorship is poised as an architectural research activity, substantially tuned with the model of research through practice that is increasingly gaining traction. This kind of research does not seek to develop new understanding from a space of pure analysis, but through generative, design activity. Rather than artificially construct an outside from which to stand apart from the subject, this is research through active, generative engagement – through both affecting and being affected.

'Before I'm an architect,' says Franch , 'I'm a citizen of the world.' But, she points out, 'I will say that I do cook as an architect, I do work as an architect, I do see and watch and listen and read as an architect.' As director of Storefront she is, in short, an architect that takes citizenship, or collective belonging, seriously. Her sense of collectivity becomes an internal as much as an external condition, dividing herself into multiple architectural roles – the facilitator, the iconographer and the agitator: 'It's important to be conscious of these three roles in every single project: to facilitate or enable people to actually express their ideas and to take their projects on; to produce projects that are representative of what I believe Storefront as an

alternative institution should be doing, and to simultaneously
shake and question the current state of affairs. The combination
of these three modes of operation converge in what I call the
figure of the utopianiser: the one invested in changing the real
nature that exists behind everything, in order to produce new
spaces of alterity. At Storefront I'm doing this mostly through
the creation of new formats of engagement and events that
try to make a very close reading of both New York, as a centre
of architectural discourse, as well as what is happening in
the discipline and society as a whole. I try to provide formats
that unveil new realities.' Across the different modalities of
engagement or roles she simultaneously adopts, Franch is 'really
trying to experiment with what constitutes a space of disruption
or innovation.'

There is something utterly singular in the extent to which
Franch is willing to experiment and take risks in and with a
public. If she stands out from the crowd, it is done *with* the
crowd – being both distinctly individual and deeply involved in
participation. Her force of personality and strength of presence
is hard to miss, becoming immediately evident through her
experiments in dressing: 'It's a game; you just play with your self,
with your life. It's taking a risk, and just seeing how materials,
how folds, how people, how things work – in order to produce a
multifaceted landscape of disruptions.'

It is easy to dismiss activities such as how one dresses as
trivial, unimportant, and of less value than more 'serious' or
weighty intellectual discourse. However, the importance of
games, play and laughter as tactics for creative research and
innovation has been noted by numerous scholars. Paulo Virno,

for instance, has discussed how 'Wit is the *diagram* of innovative
action',[3] and Arthur Koestler begins his enquiry into *The Act of
Creation* with an analysis of humour:

> The creative act of the humorist consisted in bringing about
> a momentary fusion between two habitually incompatible
> matrices. Scientific discovery ... can be described in very
> similar terms – as the permanent fusion of matrices of
> thought previously believed to be incompatible .... The
> history of science abounds with examples of discoveries
> greeted with howls of laughter because they seemed to be a
> marriage of incompatibilities – until the marriage bore fruit.[4]

Humour, innovation and spaces of disruption, share the
same diagram, where things simultaneously hold together and
remain disjunctive. When Franch discusses laughter, it is clear
that she understands its importance in terms of shared belonging
and contextual intricacies: 'When someone tells you a joke, the
moment of laughter is an act of common sense; it is an individual
process, yet it only works through a collective understanding
of language and culture. So for me, the ability to actually laugh
together is an expression of convergence, of understanding the
context, the origins and ultimately the subtleties.'

Humour, innovation and spaces of disruption, share the
same 'diagram' – all being events in which things simultaneously
hold together and remain disjunctive. As an example, Franch's
'Critical Halloween', a costume architecture party dedicated to
the theme of 'banality', was not just a dressing-up party, but 'a
way to actually provoke questions and to resonate with society

at large, in a way that otherwise would be impossible'. This event, and others such as the 'Paella Series', are ways in which she aims to 'produce a state of distraction, a state of lightness, to actually be able to reach out to the heaviest thoughts that we only throw out when we think that no one is looking, or we think that no one is listening. And I really truly believe in the value of lightness, because we are all too self conscious of who we are, of what we do, of what we say, of what we have learned off the pages of books.' Franch describes this tactic as similar to Hitchcock's plot device of the MacGuffin – dressing-up becoming a ploy or decoy that enables and motivates other goals.

If innovation has become the MacGuffin in the narratives of cultural activity, Franch employs MacGuffins to stimulate the conditions for innovation, devising ways to do much more than display or represent art and architectural culture. Across these and other frameworks, such as the 'Productive Disagreements' and 'Manifesto Series', she activates different kinds and modes of reflexivity, ways of enabling generative disruption, and thereby setting up the conditions for fostering innovative action. One might see her practice as channelling the insights of Frederick Kiesler who, as Sylvia Lavin writes, understood that:

> the effects of a storefront [are] analogous to how weather fronts are understood today as the plane of negotiation between different atmospheric densities and principal cause of meteorological phenomena. The storefront, in other words, was for Kiesler an opportunity to produce new kinds of urban happenings that might begin or be catalysed by the plane itself but that have their consequence elsewhere, out there.[5]

As a swelling of the sidewalk, Storefront presents us with a less planar, more immersive situation than Kiesler's shop window designs might have been able to offer – as active and as activating as he intended them to be.[6] Perhaps the key shift is that Franch herself operates from inside this space, like Barbarella inside the 'excessive machine' (see pp 19–21 of this issue). One might also productively relate her practice to Mark Burry's discussion on the work and contribution of Frank Pick (see pp 26–29), who also created systems whereby collective innovative design excellence was fostered, while acknowledging individual contributions. These two instigators, Pick and Franch, stand out with, through and for the vitality of the crowd, leading with an effervescent and lasting wake. ⌂

Notes
1. Eva Franch i Gilabert, 'Ecologies of Excess: An Excerpt from a 22nd-Century Architecture History Class', in Lydia Kallipoliti (ed), ⌂ *Eco-Redux*, November/December (no 6), 2010, pp 72–9.
2. This and subsequent quotes from Franch are taken from an interview with Pia Ednie-Brown, April 2012.
3. Paolo Virno, 'Wit and Innovation', trans Arianna Bove, 2004: http://eipcp.net/transversal/0207/virno/en.
4. Arthur Koestler, *The Act of Creation*, Hutchinson (London), 1969, pp 94–5.
5. Sylvia Lavin, *Kissing Architecture*, Princeton University Press (Princeton, NJ and Oxford), 2011, p 89.
6. Frederick Kiesler, *Contemporary Art Applied to the Store and its Display*, Brentano's Publishers (New York), 1930.

Veronika Valk

ARCHITECTURE AS INITIATIVE

(A MANIFESTO)

Veronika Valk, *Kultuurtuli* light installation, Tallinn Festival of Light, Tallinn, 2000
opposite: The festival takes place in the Kultuurikatel, Tallinn's cultural hub, on the site of the former heating plant complex between the city's waterfront and Old Town. The area was previously a military zone, but is now undergoing a vast transformation into spaces for the public. As an initiative, it sets out to catalyse the waterfront, where a multitude of facilities for arts and sciences are conceived as an open-study book and learning tool, to be explored and evolved over time.

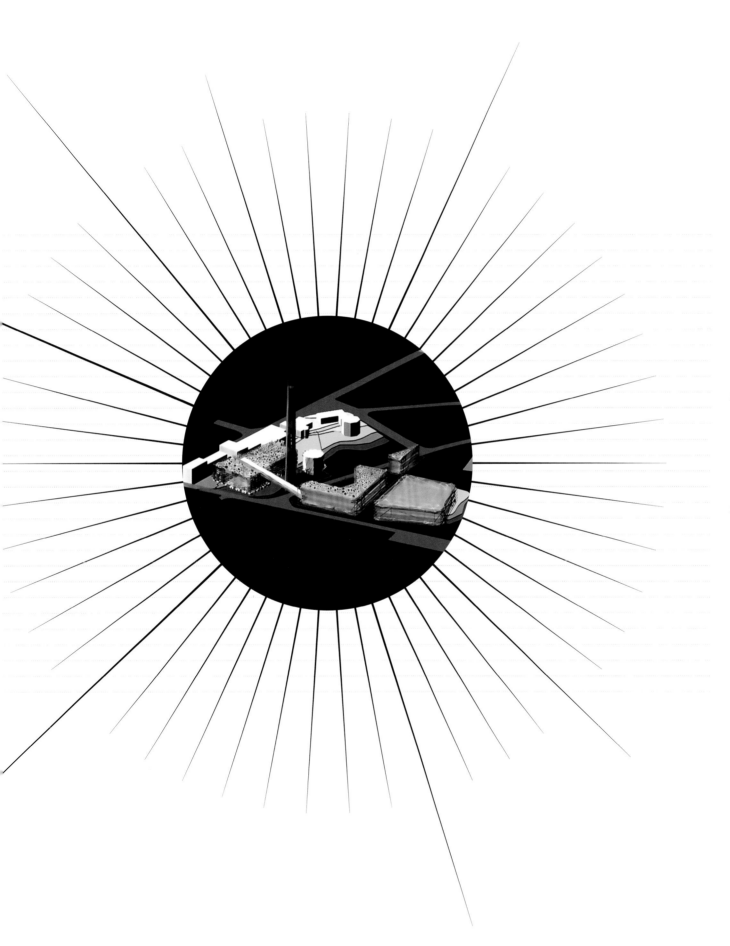

Estonian architect **Veronika Valk** of Zizi&Yoyo provides a manifesto for contemporary practice, based on 'architecture as initiative'; initiative being defined as the basic catalyst for change in a project, whether it is a small-scale art installation or an urban development. As self-contained ideas factories, initiatives generate 'open and affirmative ways to approach innovation in architecture'.

An initiative is the smallest unit of vitality in living environments – similar to the biological cell in a living organism.

Zizi&Yoyo was founded in 2005 in Tallinn, Estonia. It was initially formed by performance artist Yoko Alender and myself as a collaborative office for architecture and event-production. From 2007 onwards, the graphic designer Helene Vetik took over Alender's position in the partnership. During the course of the practice's various manifestations, an approach has been developed that might be called 'architecture as initiative'. This 'manifesto' draws on the research that we have undertaken as Zizi&Yoyo, and progresses the idea that practices, which generate 'initiative', offer potentially open and affirmative ways to approach innovation in architecture.

What is an Initiative?

An initiative is the smallest unit of vitality in living environments – similar to the biological cell in a living organism.[1] All change is brought about by an initiative, from single concepts such as a shelter or stage, as in the Mikrouun project (2006–7), to complicated urban developments such as cities, which are formed by multiple initiatives.

In its role as the basic catalyst for change, an initiative might be considered as a relatively simple collection of components in process, gently 'ticking over' to maintain itself, and occasionally propagating new initiatives. Nothing could be further from the truth.

Veronika Valk, Aili Vahtrapuu and Louis Dandrel, *Monument for Eduard Tubin*, Tartu, Estonia, 2005
Visitors can hear fragments of Estonian composer Tubin's music by knocking on the gongs on the back wall, the monument operating as an interactive soundscape installation in front of the city's main theatre.

Each and every initiative, from the simplest to the most complicated, is a self-contained ideas factory, like the molecular factory of the cell 'working frantically throughout every minute of its lifespan'.[2] This is how we can think about formations such as the Weimar Republic and Bauhaus school (1919–31), avant-garde architectural groups like Team 10 (formed at the 1953 Congrès internationaux d'architecture moderne/CIAM), Archigram (who propagated their ideas through a self-published pamphlet beginning in 1961) and Superstudio (who joined forces at the 'Superarchitettura' exhibition in Pistoia, Italy, in 1966). A 'frantic' effort is needed to maintain, nurture and evolve not only the initiative itself, but day-to-day engagement with the organisational intricacies of public bodies (such as educational and cultural institutions, government and planning authorities and so on), and the media that it touches or depends upon. Throughout its existence, much of its machinery is dismantled and rebuilt on a daily basis, ideally without any slowing of production levels. The difference between architectural practice that is not an initiator, and practice that is, is that the initiating hides within its signatures of life: processual self-replication, open-ended evolution, flocking, consciousness and the autocatalytic process that builds on itself.

One might be tempted to think of iconic architecture as initiatives; for example, the Eiffel Tower at the 1889 World's Fair in Paris, or the Skylon at the 1951 Festival of Britain. The Eiffel Tower has been the inspiration for the creation of over 30 duplicates and similar towers around the world. It has been used for TV and radio transmission, and featured in films, video games, and television shows. Yet the initiative's signatures of life have nothing to do with formal replicas or representations.

One cannot, in fact, imitate or represent an initiative. In the case of the Eiffel Tower, this was seeded by the initiative to celebrate the centennial of the French Revolution in the format of the Exposition Universelle: a World's Fair. Despite various controversies, entrepreneur-engineer Gustave Eiffel finally signed the contract with the Exposition organisers to build the tower in the knowledge that he would have to come up with three-quarters of the budget himself. The realisation of La Tour Eiffel relied on certain shared initiatives to generate the production of architecture. Such initiatives drove the 'infected' – as if carriers of an idealistic, even somewhat fanatic virus – to self-commission and mobilise diverse resources, among other things.

Initiatives, when driven by a curiosity for spatial concepts, might involve actual design

Veronika Valk, Mikrouun stage design, Kanuti Gildi SAAL, Tallinn, Estonia, 2006
The pneumatic architectural form is a space for think tanks, shows and experiments, but can also serve as a stage or urban accommodation. The Mikrouun stage, designed for the Collaboration-in-Arts international transdisciplinary laboratory (Colina Lab), was also exhibited at the 'Fête des Lumières' in Lyons, and as part of 'Another New Babylon', Cardiff, 2007.

and construction, manifestos and elaborate public debate. At a more complex level, they might start to look a lot like accelerated curating, launching explorative phenomena, such as the Tallinn Festival of Light,[3] promoting active involvement in emergent digital ecosystems and fund-raising, or implementing an array of skills in spatial arts and collaboration.

What is a Tenable Initiative?

A tenable initiative is neither solely an experiment nor an experience, but a collaborative investment, allowing something to come about – spinning off a tangent or a sideways trajectory. This requires an open mind and the desire to define without having absolute control, and the ability to express this. Sharing comes with collaboration and with chaos. This is the case for both the process of designing and how a particular project interacts with the world. For example, in the case of the *Monument for Eduard Tubin* (Tartu, Estonia, 2005), the visitor can hear fragments of Estonian composer Tubin's music by knocking on the gongs on the back wall so that the monument starts to resemble a giant drumming set. A spontaneous choreography of visitors – young and old, students and blue-collar workers – emerges when people joyfully dance back and forth, playing the gongs.

The power to initiate is a phenomenal ability that helps us bring something from nothing, and bring

it systematically. Discovery, a species of creativity, thrives on openness to difference. Working out a variety of ways to achieve something requires an ability to flexibly figure out multiple perspectives at once. Sometimes it involves the challenge of describing the indescribable. The tenable initiative is based on willingness to pursue different options, to instigate new forms of engagement with all age groups, promoting accessibility for all, or microclimates, as in *Swinging in the Light* (Tallinn, 2006). Becoming a successful initiator occurs by being oneself, and allowing for thoughts that form outside of time – for a rescaling of time in the moment of necessity.

How Can We Be Initiators Today, and Tomorrow?

Taking on many different roles during the day – designers/engineers/planners/curators/event-makers/critics/opinion leaders/artists/researchers – our practice has both internal structure and 'unstructuredness'. We need to think across scales, drilling into structural barriers with initiatives like the mobile *Pleiades Lab* for symbiotic arts and sciences (2010). This project aimed to provoke communities by initiating new ways to value (art)work that is produced in an unauthorised way. This can happen via seemingly simple architectural moves. *Pleiades* could ideally go around the world forever, as if a 'perpetuum mobile' of some sort, and still maintain

Veronika Valk, *Swinging In The Light*, Tallinn Festival of Light, Tallinn, 2006
An alternative mobile urban hotel, this installation aims at a brighter, warmer and happier wintertime by offering a different, playful use of public space in a Nordic winter streetscape. The insulated super-sized hammocks, together with an array of infrared lamps, intensify the feeling of warmth and wellbeing, inviting both locals and visitors to spend time outside, regardless of the hostile climatic conditions.

Veronika Valk, *Pleiades Lab*, hybrid lab itinerary proposal for the European Commission 7th Framework Programme, 2010
The structure acts as a hybrid agent for art and science in the public realm. It consists of six 6-metre (20-foot) shipping containers, four of which are cut in two, giving a range of configurations that can be adapted for specific sites and uses.

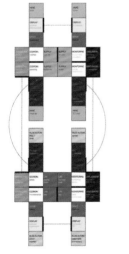

its surprise as an innovation hub by being adaptive to changing locations and their microclimates. It strives to be simultaneously temporal and permanent, poised with the question of whether we can ever escape the imperative of continuous 'progress' (which neither post-capitalism nor post-humanism seems to have achieved).

We need to remain cautious about scenarios driven by efficiency and automatic processes. Concentrating on presence, we can look for the present moment, for intimacy, the previously invisible and/or ambivalences, but also retain the condition of waiting. We can cultivate decency and guide creativity by avoiding repetition and unlimited desire. For example, the Lasva Water Tower conversion (Lasva Parish, Võru County, Estonia, 2009) started for us as a proposition for a playful concept, that of the 'piano stairs' (each step is equipped with a hammer system that hits the truss barrier to produce a specific sound, as in the keys of a piano), structured around fun, but acquired resonance among locals for its humility and simplicity.

Similar to installing the 35-storey Smotel (2000) in an 85-metre-tall disused chimney as part of the Kultuurikatel redevelopment of the old Tallinn heating plant complex, on the waterfront close to the old town and passenger harbour, we may need to retrofit our vocabulary to reach the public. Finding alternative ways to communicate and reach as many people

as possible, with whatever means and technologies are available, gives us an opportunity to shift the way we think and operate together. When we trigger and support initiatives that fascinate many through societal relevance and contagious humour, the participants, and even those who just witness others having fun, catch the mood and are encouraged to communicate their experiences, spreading the approach.

The potential of spatial arts to forge meaningful connections between people, places and attitudes – the vitality that architecture can generate, and the architecture generated through vitalising initiatives – is what it ultimately means to approach architecture as initiative. A practice dependent on initiative needs to channel this resourceful underlying current. Contagious, alive and able to self-assemble, once architecture as initiative is 'released' (realised as the built/living environment), our actions within the life of the initiative continue to matter. ᴆ

Notes
1. Terence Allen and Graham Cowling, *The Cell: A Very Short Introduction*, Oxford University Press (New York), 2011.
2. Ibid, p 1.
3. A series of installations and events in public spaces that have taken place annually since 1999 during Estonia's darkest and coldest winter months.

Veronika Valk, Kadri Klementi, Kalle-Priit Pruuden, Kalle Tikas and Peeter Laurits, Lasva Water Tower conversion, Lasva Parish, Võru County, Estonia, 2009
The main attraction of this building is the piano staircase, which can be played like a musical instrument and leads up to a grass-roof viewing platform. The project has helped to restore and strengthen a sense of identity in this remote rural community.

Veronika Valk, Smotel, Tallinn Waterfront, Tallinn, 2000
Proposal to install a 35-storey hotel in a disused brick chimney next to the Kultuurikatel. With one room per floor, guests will be able to enjoy panoramic views across Tallinn Bay and the historic city centre.

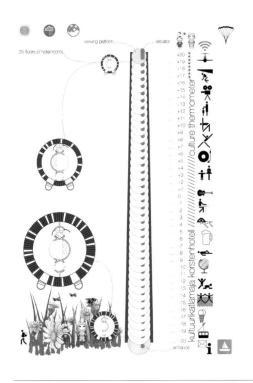

Greg Lynn FORM, Ark of the World,
Tarcoles River, Costa Rica, 2003
top: Ark of the World was conceived as a tourist
destination in the rainforest of the Tarcoles River,
having a mixed programme of natural history
museum, ecology centre and contemporary art
museum.

Greg Lynn FORM, Embryological House, 1999
bottom: Sterolith model. The Embryological House project speculated on a housing
system developable from a malleable 'primitive' geometry into a potentially unlimited
series of 'blob' iterations. These were conceived as being constructed as a monocoque
aluminium shell with secondary frame and additional steel members. Lynn's recent work
with composites examines ways in which the tectonic logic of these early propositions
could now be reconceptualised, as the Room Vehicle Prototype begins to suggest.

ON A FINE

Architectural innovators often work on the cusp
of what is feasible, acceptable and convincing.
Practising futuristically can also mean risking
going down a blind alley. Over the last two
decades, **Greg Lynn** has been one of the leading
figures in innovative practice, demonstrating an
instinct for the meaningfully inventive. One of his
major contributions has been cross-fertilisation of
technologies, introducing the likes of animation and
robotics from other disciplines into architecture.
Having interviewed Lynn in April 2012, Guest-
Editor **Pia Ednie-Brown** reflects on the specific
characteristics of his work and mode of operation.

'To do this kind of work – it's a very fine line between sounding
like you're a lunatic, and sounding like you're on the cutting edge
of architecture. It's a fine line.'[1] This is advice Greg Lynn offered
to his students during a review of a studio work exploring the
potential for robotic architectures. Proposals for robotically
activated, moving buildings, described through animations and
physically modelled using digital fabrication technologies, has
been a pursuit of Lynn's design studios for the last five years or
so. The architectural propositions are looking towards the future,
aiming for the merging of buildings and robots in ways and to
degrees that are yet to be realised. While the territory of robotic
fabrication is becoming more familiar, presenting us with new
relationships between designing and making,[2] the becoming-
robot of buildings is still 'out there'. Presumably, Lynn's advice
is that the students strive to present their propositions in ways
that come across as canny and cleverly knowing – and as such,
cutting edge rather than insane. Doing this successfully, however,
requires remaining aware that these kinds of explorations are
inevitably located on, or almost over, the edge of acceptability,
viability and believability – a bit off the beaten track, or just a bit
'off', and needing a good sniff to see if it's too far over the edge
or not.

   This edgy condition can also be where 'ugliness' sits, poised
and waiting on the edge of aesthetic insanity or 'offness'.

LINE

Pia Ednie-Brown

Greg Lynn FORM with Christian Moeller, ROOC (Robotic Operated Olympic Canopy), Olympic Park visitor attraction, London, 2009
This composite-shell canopy is supported by a series of robotic armatures, in a proposal that extends the British landscape pavilion to include interactive motion. In a state of rest, the only detectable motion of the canopy is a subtle 'breathing' quality. However, its embedded artificial life system is capable of triggering dramatic movement in response to environmental stimulus, following the sound of a passing siren or the movement of a large crowd of people as detected by its camera and microphone inputs.

GREG LYNN AND THE VOICE OF INNOVATION

Peter Eisenman seems to have felt that edge sharply, having told Lynn that his Embryological Houses were 'really ugly and horrible'. A year after making that remark, however, Lynn showed the Ark of the World museum and visitor centre project, and Eisenman found it 'disgusting', asking him: 'Why isn't it like those beautiful embryological houses?'[3] Sylvia Lavin, after having had a similar response to the visitor centre, was quoted as calling it 'the ugliest thing I ever saw'.[4] In her essay 'Freshness', she carefully attends to this issue, convincingly recasting the diagnosis of 'ugliness' in terms of novelty: 'which begins as a feeling indexically expressed convulsively and automatically in the speed of verbal utterances like "it 's ugly".'[5] Rather than being the opposite of beautiful, Lynn's architecture becomes 'something else, something other, something new'.[6] His projects, as articulated in Lavin's analysis, revive an appreciation of the aesthetic affects of novelty: maybe at first appearing mad or ugly, but in the end, as Lavin suggests, 'fresh'.

Lynn's practice has a history of innovating through cross-field technological adoption. Having famously explored the potential of animation technologies for rethinking architectural form and design technique in the 1990s, he then tweaked his trajectory towards the use of digital and other advanced fabrication technologies across many neighbouring industries, recalibrating the tropes of architectural construction, materiality and formal

languages. He is now drawing on both of these trajectories in developing projects such as ROOC (Robotic Operated Olympic Canopy), the RV (Room Vehicle) Prototype, and the Smart Mark sailing buoy, all of which quite literally and robotically move. Across these three interlinked lines of investigation, one can discern a common, intertwined attention to movement, tectonics and digitally driven machines. The way in which this attention has been directed has changed as the practice has evolved, often redefining architectural conventions along the way – shifting, for example, the logics of tectonics, construction and materials with projects like Blobwall (2005), and relations between form and structure in his use of composite materials in projects such as the more recent RV Prototype.

But what is this 'kind of work' Lynn refers to in his advice? Certainly one could give it many names – like 'innovative', 'fresh' or 'ugly' – but what are the qualities of action that mobilise it? How might we characterise the inherent approaches that make it the 'kind' that it is? If Lynn's work is innovative, which seems as widely accepted a prognosis as its ugliness, then what diagram of practice underscores this perpetual novelty machine?

We could start by pointing to Lynn's wide range of attention: 'I spend a lot of energy staying connected with people in other fields who are using a similar medium … I think of the new as being located and somehow shared between these different

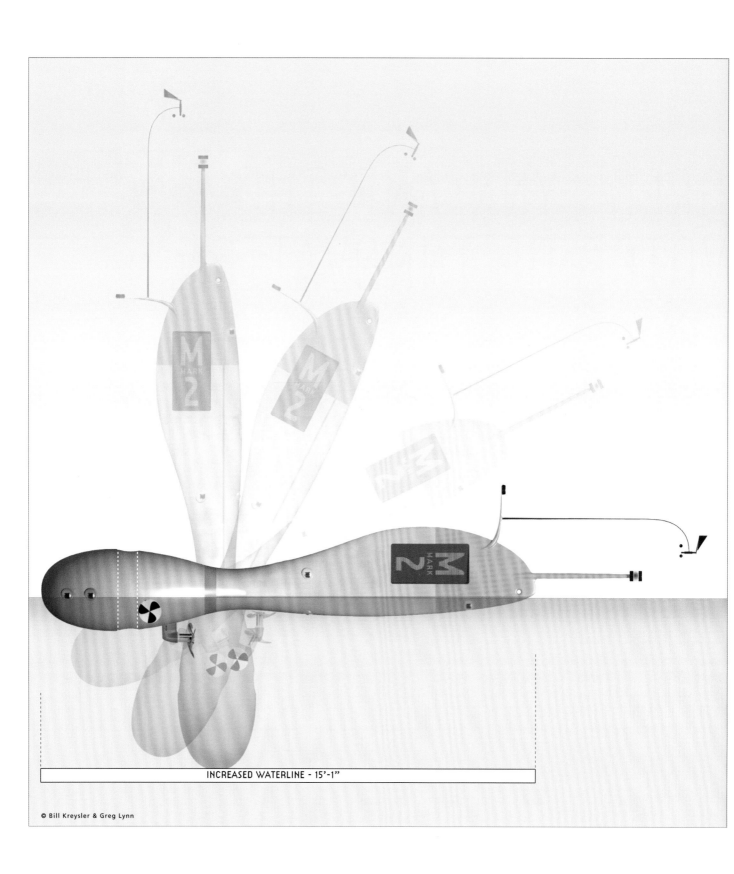

INCREASED WATERLINE - 15'-1"

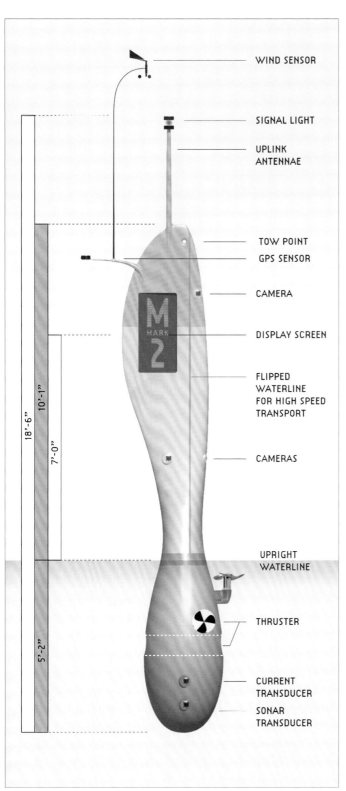

WIND SENSOR

SIGNAL LIGHT

UPLINK
ANTENNAE

TOW POINT

GPS SENSOR

CAMERA

DISPLAY SCREEN

FLIPPED
WATERLINE
FOR HIGH SPEED
TRANSPORT

CAMERAS

UPRIGHT
WATERLINE

THRUSTER

CURRENT
TRANSDUCER

SONAR
TRANSDUCER

18'-6"
10'-1"
7'-0"
5'-2"

Greg Lynn FORM

KREYSLER & ASSOCIATES

SMART MARK
INTELLIGENT BUOY

KREYSLER & ASSOCIATES
501 Green Island Road
American Canyon, CA 94503
(707) 552-3500 tel
bill@kreysler.com
www.kreysler.com

GREG LYNN FORM
1817 Lincoln Blvd.
Venice, CA 90291
(310) 821-2629 tel
(310) 430-0226 cell
greg@glform.com

REVISIONS
DATE: COMMENTS:

DATE: JANUARY 2012
FORMAT: 11" x 17"

SMART MARK

01

Greg Lynn FORM with Kreysler & Associates,
Smart Mark, 2012
A number of sensors, cameras and monitors extend
the capabilities and role of the sailing buoy. Smart
Mark can flip its orientation, creating an improved hull
profile for towing or self-propulsion.

Greg Lynn FORM, Blobwall, Los Angeles, 2005
Brightly coloured, hollow plastic rotation-moulded blobs are used in a modular system that reinvents the idea of the brick wall.

fields. You find the place where people are moving in a direction which you wouldn't see if you just only talked to all the other architects.'[7] Across Lynn's history, his practice has engaged with a diversity of collaborations and clients[8] that reflect his practice location in the Hollywood-infused West Coast of the US, plugged into entertainment and software communities. Collaborations range from Brad Pitt and motion graphics company Imaginary Forces, to major cultural institutions such as the Guggenheim Museum, jewellery company Atelier Swarovski, and composite materials manufacturer Kreysler & Associates with sailmaker North Sails. The polyphony of conversations this indicates involves more than just attention to talking with other people, which generally involves a relatively straightforward use of language. More generally, inhabiting transdisciplinary territory – getting inside alternative techniques and frameworks in order to produce the 'fresh' – requires tapping into some kind of abstraction in order to generate connections beneath, across and between the differences.

Lynn has discussed such an abstract connector in terms of 'machine language': 'Everyone in my studio knows how to talk to machines. We spend a great deal of time speaking their language, and their language is translated much more easily than ours … The spread of machine language and programming is in some ways more significant than the worldwide spread of English.'[9] One might imagine that a bunch of architects uttering machine language, talking to robots in code, could appear like a conglomerate of lunatics speaking in idiomorphic dialects.[10] But programming is only one aspect of talking to machines, also requiring an understanding of their tendencies and capacities that builds up through a history of engagement – where they fail, their limits, their capacities. Like learning to play a musical instrument and writing music for it, learning to speak with one's instrument is not just about the musical score; it involves gradually finessing one's engagement with it until you can work imaginatively with the potential it offers. As such, while virtuosos might be found muttering madly in incomprehensible tongues, they are also cleverly making cunning moves inside their engagement with instruments, like Barbarella folding the traits of the 'excessive machine' back into itself (see 'The Ethics of the Imperative' on pp 19–21 of this issue).

The virtuoso points to the idea that one's approach to engagement and negotiation within the actions of practice shapes the nature of that practice. Having engaged with many different systems, tools and techniques across an array of collaborations, there has been no lack of dance partners with which to explore and adapt different steps and movement routines. This is no small point, for as Mark Rakatansky once pointed out: 'Diagrammatics … will only be recognisable by

I spend a lot of energy staying connected with people in other fields who are using a similar medium … I think of the new as being located and somehow shared between these different fields.

Greg Lynn FORM with Kreysler & Associates, Smart Mark, 2012
Blurring distinctions between robots and objects, Smart Mark incorporates a number of new technologies to the design of a sailing buoy. These include the ability to set and adjust courses during a race, and hold position in rough seas and high currents without anchors.

The joints and connections of the blobs are cut with precision by a robot. This enables the modular wall to avoid mortar or glue, the units being welded together with a tool used to repair car bumpers.

Having engaged with many different systems, tools and techniques across an array of collaborations, there has been no lack of dance partners with which to explore and adapt different steps and movement routines.

virtue of how they are drawn forth in the act of responding to internal and external forces.'[11] An emphasis on Lynn's generosity of engagement is discussed in the essay that follows, which is an excerpt from a text written by philosopher Brian Massumi in 2000. Through closely examining the internal tendencies of the generative design techniques Lynn brought to table in the 1990s, Massumi explores the intricacies of Lynn's early work in proposing it as 'directly an ethics as a design endeavour: an ethics of engagement'. This ethics – 'constitutionally accepting of what lies outside its control, tending from the very beginning towards productive engagement' – is at the core of the virtuosity that defines what 'kind of work' Lynn's practice stands for.

Perhaps the ways that Lynn's future robotic buildings move and engage with the world will act out a movement-diagram of an implicit ethics that can be traced from the blobs, and unfolded across the subsequent production of families of buildings and objects. Might this tell us something more tangible, even if abstractly, about what 'kind of work' this is? Probably, but any such diagram of practice will be found balanced on a very fine line, not just between lunacy and the cutting edge, but between multiple polarities. If the future more explicitly unfolds the ethics that Massumi refers to, it will pertain to virtuosity rather than the virtuous, always teetering on the edge, on a fine line.[12] ⌂

Notes
1. From the video 'Giant Robot', Studio Lynn, University of Applied Arts Vienna, 2008: www.youtube.com/watch?feature=player_embedded&v=XSdXnmq37x0.
2. See Iain Maxwell and Dave Pigram, 'In the Cause of Architecture: Traversing Design and Making', *Log* 25, Summer 2012, pp 31–40.
3. Quotes from Greg Lynn interview with Pia Ednie-Brown, April 2012.
4. Sylvia Lavin, 'Freshness', in Greg Lynn, *Greg Lynn Form*, Rizzoli (New York), 2008, p 14.
5. Ibid, p 21.
6. Ibid, p 19.
7. From Greg Lynn interview with Pia Ednie-Brown, April 2012.
8. See mapping of clients and collaborators up until 2008: *Greg Lynn Form*, op cit, pp 169–70.
9. Greg Lynn, 'Machine Language', *Log* 10, Summer/Fall 2007, pp 55–63.
10. See Ezio Blasetti, 'pars (orationis)', *Log* 25, Summer 2012, pp 71–7.
11. Mark Rakatansky, 'Motivations of Animation', *Any 23: Diagram Work*, 1998, p 55.
12. See also Pia Ednie-Brown, 'Architecture on Wire: Resilience Through Vitality', *Log* 25, Summer 2012, pp 15–22.

Greg Lynn FORM, RV (Room Vehicle) Prototype, 2012
Within the footprint of a small building is a huge quantity of liveable surface. The RV Prototype rotates in both the vertical and horizontal axes, tumbling the inhabitant in something of a cross between a theme park ride, exercise machine and natural landscape. This opens up more useable surfaces: living spaces on one side, bathing on another, with sleeping above.

Brian Massumi

BECOMING ARCHITECTURAL

AFFIRMATIVE CRITIQUE, CREATIVE INCOMPLETION

When Greg Lynn embraced digital animation software in the 1990s, he not only redefined architectural production, but also the designer's relationship to the generative process. In this extract from an unpublished essay written in 2000, the philosopher **Brian Massumi** describes Lynn's 'in-folding' open-ended approach, which renders the design process 'less an external conduit for the artist's creativity' than the artist 'a conduit for creativity of the design process'.

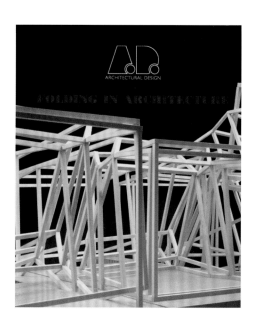

Greg Lynn (ed), ⌀ **Folding in Architecture, January 1993**
This issue of ⌀, guest-edited by Lynn, was a founding moment in emergent, or generative, design. The static geometry of Platonic solids is replaced by the curvilinear geometry of topological transformations.

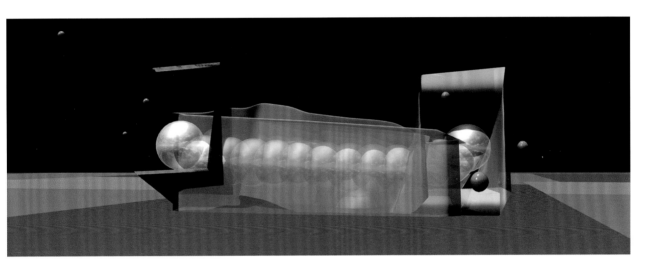

When Greg Lynn launched the rallying cry
of 'folding in architecture'[1] back in the 1990s,
he generated a tremendous amount of anxiety
and even anger over what has repeatedly
been characterised as an 'over-enthusiastic'
and 'uncritical' approach. Peter Eisenman
railed that architects like Lynn were trying to
mire the discipline in their own 'cybernetic
hallucinations'.[2] What most irked Eisenman is
precisely what Lynn rejoiced in: the blurring
of the boundary between the creature and the
creator that the new generative techniques
afforded. Failing to maintain the separation
between the powerful new tool of the trade, the
trade itself, and the creative artist amounted,
for Eisenman, to a delusional abdication of
architectural authorship. To be used responsibly,
the computer-assisted topological figure must
be kept at arm's length, on a self-reflective leash.
Its proper employment was as a mediating
device inserted between the 'authorial subject',
the authored architectural 'object', a 'receiving
subject', and the 'interiority' of architecture
as a discipline, in such a way as to maintain
their distance from each other even as it brings
them into contact. The point for Eisenman
seemed to be that the contact remain external
and regulated, so that the authorial subject may
'overcome' and 'access'. In other words, a critical
distance must be maintained.

If Lynn eschewed critical distance, he did
so by showing how design process evolves most
decidedly by integrating external constraints,
converting them into internal growth factors:
folding them into its self-generative activity.
The process is additive and affirmative. It
is capable not only of multiplying versions
of its formal results *ad infinitum*, but also of
indefinitely increasing and varying the internal
variables it eventfully combines towards each
result. Welcoming of intrusion from outside,
such a process is 'pliant'. Which is not the same
as 'compliant'. It does not conform to external
constraints. It folds them in – to its own
unfolding. It uses them to vary its results, to
creatively diverge. Both in terms of its internal
disposition and its outward responsiveness,
the process more fundamentally involves a
composition of relations than of forms or
elements of form. The 'in-folding' approach

Greg Lynn FORM, House Prototype in
Long Island, New York, 1994
An iterative series of models is generated
by adjusting parameters. The design is
evolutionary. A proliferation of variations
is generated from which a well-adapted
selection is made.

Lynn's trademark was 'blobs'. The blob modelling
program he used was Wavefront Technology's
Meta-Balls, part of its Explorer 3Design program,
hijacked by Lynn from its intended use in Hollywood
animation in what was to prove a founding gesture
of digital architecture.

invites the desires and values of others, among
other alien 'constraints', to feature as positive
occasions for growth. This is a welcoming
approach to design, constitutionally accepting
of what lies outside its control, tending from the
very beginning towards productive engagement.
'Folding-in' architecture is as directly an ethics
as a design endeavour: an ethics of engagement.

Lynn's trademark was 'blobs'. The blob
modelling program he used was Wavefront
Technology's Meta-Balls, part of its Explorer
3Design program, hijacked by Lynn from its
intended use in Hollywood animation in what
was to prove a founding gesture of digital
architecture. A blob is a flexible sphere radiating
a quasi-gravitational field of influence. The
force of the field varies according to the blob's
surface area and assigned 'mass'. When two or
more blobs enter into proximity, their fields of
influence interact, forming a zone of relation or
reciprocal transformation. Depending on how
their relation plays, they will either inflect each
other's surface amoebically in unpredictable
ways, or fuse into a single super-blob. From
the topological point of view, Lynn notes, a
sphere is but a lonely blob: a 'blob without
influence', isolated from neighbouring forces.[3]
Classical geometric figures can be considered
isolates or extractive limit-cases of topological
transformations. Now put a gaggle of blobs
in a gradient field and let the program run.
The blobs will stretch around each other like
amorous slugs. Some will fuse, forming pluri-
chambered bulbous structures or tubulations.
What collective shape arises from their
deformational congress cannot be predicted
with accuracy. The blobs do not only mutually
deform; their reciprocal transformation is
itself inflected by the surrounding gradient
field. Relation of relation. Interrelation to the
second power: greater complexity, increased
unforeseeability. Stop the program. The

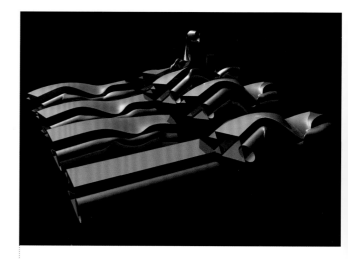

visible shape you are left with is a processual
emergence from the relationally unforeseen.

Suppose the shape is earmarked to become
a house. But suppose the client does not want
to live in the stomach of a highly unforeseen
amoeba. Say the client wants a house of a
certain generic floor plan. An H-plan, for
example. This was the external typological
constraint placed on Lynn's House Prototype
in Long Island project (1994).[4] Lynn realised
that blobular stretching and fusing, or other
too random form-generating procedures, could
be limited by addition: by adding another
relationality. Blobs were attached to an H-frame
made of 'splines'. A spline structure is composed
of linear segments attached end to end to
form a 'skeleton'. Unlike a Euclidean line
drawing, the spline figure is active. The points
of intersection between skeletal segments have
virtual strings attached to them. The strings
are vectors pulling on each intersection in a
different direction, with variable strength. The
static figure is in fact a holding pattern formed
by a tensile equilibrium between vectorial forces
differentially applied through the length of the

Greg Lynn FORM, Port Authority Triple
Bridge Gateway, competition entry,
1994
top: This project was the first in design
history to use animation software for the
generation of architectural form.

bottom: Traffic and pedestrian circulation
were modelled as site forces using
animations of particle flows. The changing
paths of the particles in response to the
forces suggested architectural solutions
optimising circulation.

frame. If you vary the strength of one of the vectors, the influence propagates throughout the entire skeleton. The frame moves like the X-ray of a mime. Although compositionally the spline frame is linear and segmented, the movement that propagates through its structure is continuous and curved. The activation of the tensile relation between linear segments describes a topological transformation. A spline frame is a Euclidean figure whose activation generates topological effects.

In the Long Island House project, the virtual strings attached to the intersection points of the splinar H-frame connected to 'site forces': attractions or repulsions in the gradient field modelling the plot on which the house would be built. Again in response to client preference, the site forces primarily concerned visibility. A large tree and the line of sight to the ocean were programmed as forces of attraction. A neighbouring house blocking the view of the ocean and an existing driveway were forces of repulsion. The connection of the skeleton frame to these forces actively translated features of the site into form. To be more

precise, they translated values attached to site features into iterations of proto-architectural form generation. The values entering the process, it must be emphasised, were not the architect's. The architect's contribution came in the way a formal typology and hierarchy of values imposed by another's desires were integrated into the developing design process.

The blobs seem to have their own desires. They have attached themselves to certain edges of the frame. While the frame is busy formally propagating translated site influences, the blobs are at it again, doing their amoebic mating dance. But their range of amoebic mutation was now limited by their value-laden splinal mooring. Their neighbourly abandon is moderated in a way that successfully renders it proto-functional: the tubularities that the blobs become in congress will be architecturally rendered as transitional spaces between the inside of the relationally activated frame and the influential outside of site-specific values. The project, however, is never built. It remains a proto-house, its growth stopped short of actual architectural rendering.

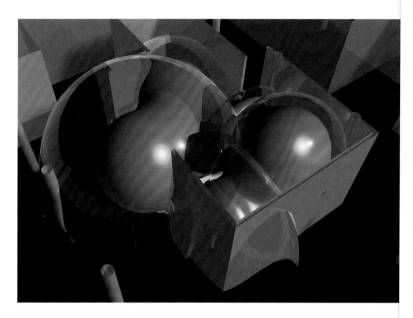

In Lynn's approach, what the architect
works with during the design process is not an
architectural object – yet. It is a proto-formal,
proto-functional, abstractly real evolutionary
entity. It is proto-architectural until it is
actually built. Animate architecture posits a
difference in kind between proto-type and
finished architectural form. The proto-type is
its own abstract reality becoming architectural.
The prefix 'proto-' is misleading. The prototype is not an already-architectural object of a
certain type waiting passively on screen to be
realised in steel. It is already actively real and
still in process: it has the virtual reality of what
might be called a hyper-type. Here, 'hyper-' can
substitute for 'proto-'.

Looking at Lynn's early design projects,
it was difficult to make sense of them as
determinate kinds of building, house or
transportation terminal (Yokahama Port
Terminal, 1994). They still had to be rendered
recognisably architectural. This happened
gradually as (if) they passed into construction.
They are architecturally typecast in passing: in
continuation of a process that changes its nature

as it goes. Its continuability is so open-ended
that even the 'completed' building will have
to be considered essentially provisional. A
built outcome could just as well have been any
number of other buildings, if the programming
and negotiated re-programmings had, by
chance of chaotic circumstance, run slightly
differently. The building retains an element of
the generic, even in its concrete particularity.
The finality of the design is by nature deferred.
There is no one moment where the architect
can stand back from the process and say: 'I,
creative master, have spoken in my form; read
what I have said.' The design process is less
an external conduit for the artist's creativity
than the artist is a conduit for creativity of the
design process.

The evolving, hyper-typological, proto-
reality of the design entity is what makes
it necessary to speak of the design process
encountering its own discipline as its outside.
The design process encounters its discipline
as an external cultural constraint or natural
given that it variationally internalises – as part
of the same passage by which it comes to be
internalised by the discipline, as part of its own
continuing variation (double becoming).

But is not this true of any design process,
topological or otherwise? If design were
architecturally predefined, how could designing
change architecture? How would architecture
itself ever evolve? It would be trapped in the
vicious circle of its definition preceding itself,
only ever to become what it already is. The very
fact that architecture has a history necessitates
the paradoxical view of the design process as a
real becoming integratively outside the history
it changingly enters.

What was new and different about animate
architecture was neither its virtuality – its self-
immanent proto-reality – nor its co-variational
emergence. What was new is that it admitted
to and nurtured them; that it admitted to
being just emergent (rather than always already
defined); that it brought out its coming out and
revelled in it, taking cheer in its own creative
incompletion. Never did Lynn claim to be the
end-all. The would-be manifesto announced by
Sanford Kwinter and Jeffrey Kipnis for unveiling
at the 1998 Any Conference in Rotterdam was
a confirmation of this. A promised manifesto
heralding an apocalyptic end to the architecture
of the elders and claiming animate architecture
as the generational dawning of a new age simply
failed to materialise, stranding Kwinter on stage
awkwardly presenting its incompletion to an
expectant public. The manifesto never evolved
past the stage of a promise. In a way, was it not
the inability of the manifesto to evidence itself

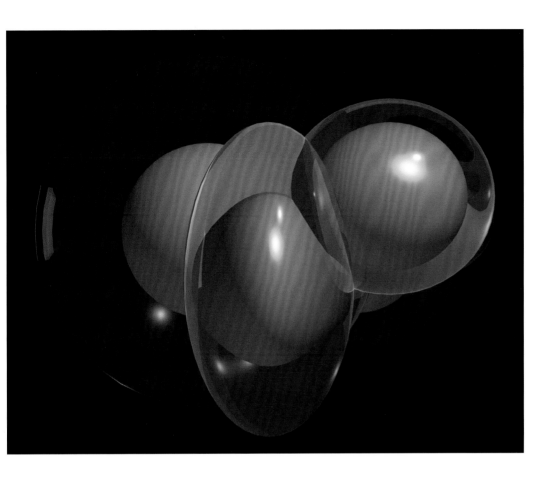

Blobs are given various weightings that respond to the proximity of other blobs, resulting in deformations of their surfaces, or their amalgamation into a larger super-blob.

that kept the promise of animate architecture? The unmanifesto: the performance, in spite of itself, of critical open-endedness.[5]

While the critical architect is required to be painfully literate – expert at 'reading' what is 'written' in visual form – the virtually affirmative architect is encouraged to be abundantly iterate. The critical architect, feeling tradition bound and hating it, is challenged by perceived strictures. The affirmative architect, operating with joyful abandon in an open relational field, is challenged by the plethora of invisible procedural possibilities.

The cheer of becoming, open-ended, challenged architecture at large to review its disciplinary being. This was not a question of revisionism. It was not a question of opposing one version of architectural history to another. The issue was the very manner in which architecture, as a discipline, has a history. Bringing out that issue is the affirmative version of critique (practised, as always, in passing). Incompletion and continuation are two sides of the same coin. Taking cheer in its own incompletion is a way of topological design to reiterate: it continues. Architecture does not only have a history. It has a future. Change ahead. ⌂

This article is an excerpt from an unpublished essay written in 1999.

The design process encounters its discipline as an external cultural constraint or natural given that it variationally internalises.

Notes
1. Greg Lynn (ed), ⌂ *Folding in Architecture*, first edition, January 1993; second edition, with a new introductory essay by Mario Carpo, 2003.
2. Peter Eisenman, 'Diagram: An Original Scene of Writing', *Diagram Diaries*, Thames & Hudson (London), 1999, p 27. Republished in Mark Garcia (ed), *The Diagrams of Architecture: ⌂ Reader*, John Wiley & Sons (London), 2010, p 96.
3. Greg Lynn, *Folds, Bodies and Blobs: Collected Essays*, La Lettre Volée (Brussels), 1998, p 166.
4. Greg Lynn, *Animate Form*, Princeton Architectural Press (New York), 1999, pp 142–63.
5. See Cynthia Davidson (ed), *Anyhow*, MIT Press (Cambridge, MA), 1999.

THE EBB AND FLOW OF DIGITAL INNOVATION

Mario Carpo

Michael Hensel and Achim Menges, Form finding and dynamic relaxation: Membrane Morphologies 02, Diploma Unit 4, Architectural Association (AA), London, 2005
Close-up view of 'minimal hole' configuration. The Emergence and Design Group (Michael Hensel, Achim Menges and Michael Weinstock) was a pioneer in the investigation of the notion of 'emergence' and of the mathematical, rather than holistic and intuitive, design strategies deriving from it.

Architectural historian and theorist **Mario Carpo** examines the status quo of digital innovation. Whereas the espousal of animation software in the 1990s placed architects conspicuously at the forefront of new technologies as early adopters and adapters, in the new millennium they have less enthusiastically embraced the participatory opportunities of Web 2.0 and open-source modes of working. Could the desire for single authorship be holding designers back?

FROM FORM MAKING TO FORM FINDING – AND BEYOND

There was a time, not long ago, when
architecture was at the forefront of digital
innovation. For sure, architects and
designers did not invent digital technology –
they just adopted and adapted it, borrowing
animation software from the film industry or
CAD-CAM technology from aircraft makers,
for example. But in the 1990s architects
and designers gave visible form to the
digital age. An unprecedented architectural
experience, the new aesthetics of free form
soon also became a source of technological
education for all. Free form represented
and symbolised a new techno-cultural
environment where all the tenets of industrial
Modernism had been jettisoned, and a
new universe of differentiation, variation,
and choice – which Postmodernism had
advocated, but could not deliver – became
possible, tangible, affordable and, some
claim, even pleasurable. In the process,
architects and designers contributed to
some significant technological advances,
and digital design theory in the 1990s set
the trends for digital thinking at large.

Then came the dotcom crash, and early
in the new century the digital economy
reinvented itself along the lines of the so-
called Web 2.0 – the participatory Web.
Architects, for the most part, did not take
notice. For them, participation was nothing
new, and nothing to be excited about. Digital
parametricism is collaborative by its very
technical nature, and all designers knew
and know it. But the participatory use of
digital technologies is a highly disruptive
cultural and technical paradigm; the music
and film industries have already learned this
to their detriment, and some of the subtler
interpreters of digital culture these days
are not media critics or technologists, but
intellectual property (IP) lawyers.[1] Architecture
as we know it – an allographic, notational
art of design that replaced building as a
mechanical craft at the end of the Middle
Ages – is part of the early modern invention
of humanistic authorship, and a new technical
paradigm that is inherently anti-authorial, and
collaborative by its nature, is unlikely to be
friendly to architects. There is no need to be
a Renaissance specialist to sense that few
architects are willing to stop designing to
become managers of the design intentions of
others – never mind the degree of technical
sophistication now offered by digital crowd-
sourcing.

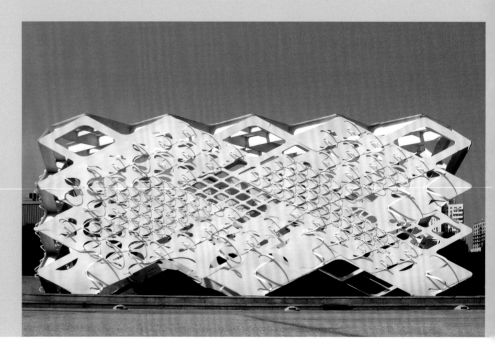

This may be one reason why the participatory turn in digital design never happened: digital design never went 2.0. Designers are for the most part oblivious of, if not hostile to, the participatory potential embedded in the technical logic of all things digital, including the very same digital tools they use. Some digital designers pride themselves on using open-source software, but few or none use digital tools to design open-sourceable architecture: that is, to author open-ended parametric notations that other sub-authors, co-authors or interactors could customise, edit or modify at will. The one distinctly Web 2.0 application for architecture, building information modelling (BIM), is not popular among the design professions. Driven by the technical logic of digital data management, BIM software envisages and favours a strongly anti-authorial and participatory design environment and, not surprisingly, architects often see it as a ploy of the building and construction industry, and a potential enemy of their authorial status.[2]

This is where digital culture and the design professions seem to have taken different paths, with digital design losing its innovative edge – even its capacity to reinvent itself – in the process. It is as difficult to get excited about a *soi-disant* innovative theory which, for the last 10 years, has been repeating arguments that for the most part are 20 years old, as it is difficult to empathise with a *soi-disant* cutting-edge style that advocates the permanent and universal repetition of a spline-driven design environment, most of which also dates from the early 1990s. Yet, despite this dull and unpromising backdrop, at the borderline between design, materials science and structural engineering, one area of high-tech design is still witnessing the pristine thrill and excitement of novelty and discovery. It has been known for a while that digital technologies make it increasingly possible to analyse and predict the structural behaviour of many hitherto intractable, 'irregular' (unelastic, anisotropic) materials, natural as well as artificial. And as digitally intelligent designers seem to have shifted their focus, accordingly, from the design of non-standard geometries of form to the design of non-standard materials and structures, a new and quite peculiar approach to structural form finding, endorsed by many architects as well as by some noted engineers, seems to be fast gaining appeal and recognition.

Digital design theory has been marked from its beginnings by the so-called Postmodern science of indeterminacy and by related theories of complexity, chaos and non-linearity. The morphogenetic approach to digital design has been a fertile ground for this kind of speculation; whether genetic or mathematical, code is code, and as evolution appears to happen by natural selection in biology, many have argued that the same may happen in computation. When applied to structural and material systems, this metaphor favours the belief that at times inert matter may, simply put, come alive. Living matter, then, does what it wants, and finds whatever is best for itself and by itself: matter, just like nature, at times chooses to 'self-organise', by definition in unpredictable ways. If this assumption may appear improbable, in the etymological sense of being difficult to prove, it may not be more difficult to prove than its opposite; vitalism has a long and distinguished tradition in the history of Western thought, and on the other hand, many perfectly functioning alternatives to predictive sciences are currently used by technologists and scientists who most certainly do not see themselves as animists, voodooists or magicians.[3]

Architecture as we know it ... is part of the early modern invention of humanistic authorship, and a new technical paradigm that is inherently anti–authorial, and collaborative by its nature, is unlikely to be friendly to architects.

Michael Hensel and Achim Menges,
Form finding and dynamic relaxation
Membrane Morphologies 02, Diploma Unit
4, Architectural Association (AA), London,
2005
Initial form-finding experiment of 'minimal hole'
configuration.

Digital simulation can make and break more models in a few seconds than a traditional craftsman could in a lifetime, thus making intuitive, heuristic form finding by trial and error a perfectly viable design strategy.

But architects often need to simplify complex theories to adapt them to their daily chores, and in architectural discourse the Postmodern theories of non-linearity are often translated into the blunter assumption that the structural behaviour of some material systems (the way they deform under load, for example) may at times be just impossible to predict causally, either because our science is not good enough, or because no science can predict the intentions of nature. Either way, the traditional, analytical mode of structural design (born from 19th-century positivism and mathematics) is thus proclaimed extinct, and a new discipline ushered in, in its stead, where forms are not designed but 'found', by holistic intuition or intellection, and by dint of a mute and tacit empathy between the maker and the materials being crafted. This mode of 'design by making', always a popular one among designers, replaces design and calculation with craft and intuition, now complemented and vindicated by the power of computer modelling: digital simulation can make and break more models in a few seconds than a traditional craftsman could in a lifetime, thus making intuitive, heuristic form finding by trial and error a perfectly viable design strategy.[4]

Holistic engineering is a vast and challenging field of investigation, where high-tech and hocus-pocus, science and belief, design agendas and political ideologies often merge and overlap. As the digital craftsmen of a new generation come of age, eagerly testing the digital re-enactments of many ancestral, gestural traces of hand-making, it is worth noting that digital form finding invites a drastic redefinition of agency, not dissimilar from that which characterises the Web 2.0 at large. In both ambits, digital tools favour and foster the elimination of humanistic and modern authorship: in one case, to the advantage of unpredictable social actors and networks; in the other, to the advantage of the equally unpredictable forces of nature and of their capacity to evolve and self-organise. In the social version of the Web 2.0, designers may become curators of the choices of others. In the naturalistic version of holistic form finding, designers become the midwives of emerging natural powers. Form finders do not design or determine form in the traditional way; emergent forms may be seconded, favoured or encouraged, but at the end of the day they just happen.[5]

Co-designing with nature, negotiating with and even surrendering to nature's will and whim are timeless human ambitions, powerfully redefined in the industrial age by 19th-century romanticism and by the various naturalisms and organicisms that followed in the course of the 20th century. As our worldview is being dramatically redefined by the inescapable perception of the limits of human making and of the finiteness of our environment, one can see many reasons why the quest for a renewed alliance with nature may seem a wiser and more urgent policy today than at any time in modern history. But in the Western, humanistic tradition, design was often meant to be the making of a visible, not of an invisible hand, whether this invisible hand be nature's own, or the hand of any other self-organising system; and it would be puzzling, and also worrisome, if today's designers had agreed to interpret and develop the power of the new technologies in a way that abets, furthers and praises what some like to portray as the random agency of chaos. Complexity and chaos are very different notions. We may choose to favour self-organisation and digital Darwinism in design, but let us not fool ourselves: we already know what social Darwinism has in mind. ⌀

Notes
1. See, for example, Lawrence Lessig's discussion of 'copylefting' and other digital alternatives to analogue copyright laws, recently republished in Lawrence Lessig, 'Re-Crafting a Public Domain', *Perspecta 44 – Domain: The Yale Architectural Journal*, 2011, pp 177–89.
2. Mario Carpo, 'Epilogue: Split Agency', *The Alphabet and the Algorithm*, MIT Press (Cambridge, MA), 2011, pp 123–28; Mario Carpo, 'Digital Style', *Log* 23, 2011, pp 41–52; and Mario Carpo, 'Introduction', *The Digital Turn in Architecture, 1992–2012: ⌀ Reader*, John Wiley & Sons (London), 2012.
3. The best account of the architectural interpretations of 'non-linearity' and their intellectual provenance is in Charles Jencks, *The Architecture of the Jumping Universe: A Polemic – How Complexity Science is Changing Architecture and Culture*, Academy (London), 1995. See also ⌀ *New Science = New Architecture*, September/October (no 9/10), 1997, guest-edited by Charles Jencks. On the architecture of 'emergence', see the works of members of the former Emergence and Design Group (Michael Hensel, Achim Menges and Michael Weinstock), starting with the seminal ⌀ *Emergence: Morphogenetic Design Strategies*, May/June (no 3), 2004, guest-edited by the same.
4. See Mario Carpo, 'Digital Darwinism', *Log* 26, 2012, and 'Thunder on the Horizon', *Fulcrum: The AA's Weekly Free Sheet* 47, 6 June 2012.
5. For some different views, see *Log* 25, Summer 2012, guest-edited by François Roche, where the term 'form finding' is used by different authors in different contexts, sometimes to denote causal processes of mathematical optimisation (which fall outside the ambit of this article).

Emergence: form and indeterminacy in nature
below top: According to Michael Weinstock, who published this image in his seminal book, *The Architecture of Emergence* (John Wiley & Sons, 2010), the rising bubbles of steam in boiling water show some of the characteristics of emergence: the general configuration of the system at boiling temperature is precisely predictable, but the position or form of any individual bubble of steam is not.

Frank Gehry, Guggenheim Museum, Bilbao, under construction, circa 1996
below bottom: Iconic digital form making in the 1990s.

Pia Ednie-Brown

STRANGE VITALITY

THE TRANSVERSAL ARCHITECTURES OF MOS AND NEW TERRITORIES/R&SIE(N)

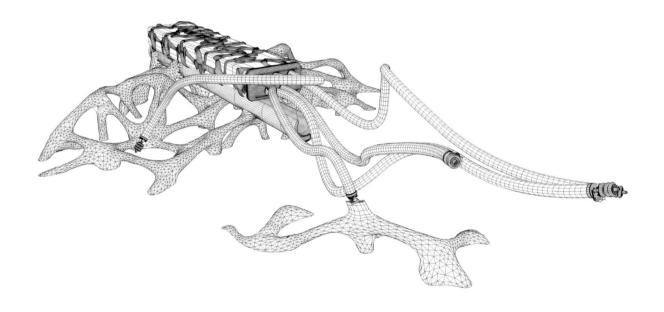

New Territories/R&Sie(n), 'I've heard about', 2005
Image sequence speculating on a robotic, algorithmically driven process through which an urban structure is built, or grows, based on contingencies of an ever-emerging and shifting sociality. The exhibition at the Musée d'Art Moderne, Paris (2005) presented a series of digital and physical scale models of urban structures arising from such a system, with the *Hypnochamber* as a 1:1 built prototype of a potential fragment of this construction.

Guest-Editor **Pia Ednie-Brown** provides a foil to Mario Carpo's discussion of digital innovation. She argues for an emerging 'strange vitality' in contemporary computational design that is highly innovative: being disruptive rather than incremental in the manner in which it seeks out innovation. She specifically describes how MOS (Michael Meredith and Hilary Sample) and New Territories/ R&Sie(n), led by François Roche, are reinventing digital design in architecture by reconnecting it through a variety of media to broader cultural and social issues.

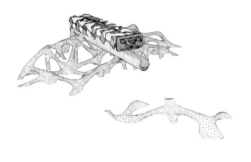

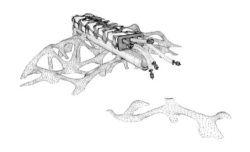

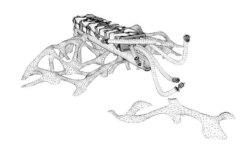

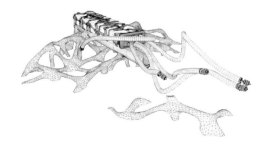

R&Sie(n) portrait
This digital portrait of R&Sie(n) is a morphed combination of its three members (François Roche, Stéphanie Lavaux and Gilles Desevedavy) – a digital hermaphrodite that stood in for photographs of any members of the practice. They have discussed this as a way to dis-identify themselves, a strategy of de-personalising.

MOS, *Glimmering Noise: Notes for those Beginning the Discipline of Architecture*, film still, 2005
In this film, Professor Michael Meredith is on stage being interviewed in front of a silent but live audience by a critic who pompously derides architects and architecture, persistently talking over Meredith. Sporting a neck brace, speaking with uncertainty, and often responding with only awkward silence, Meredith paints a portrait of the architectural professor as an agreeable and smart but powerless victim of discourse. This kind of architectural pathos and humour runs across many of MOS's films, which operate to both extend and critique architectural discourse and culture.

Is digital design in architecture – as Mario Carpo suggests in his article on pp 56–61 of this issue – really 'losing its innovative edge – even its capacity to reinvent itself'? In the last 10 years, he writes, this area 'has been repeating arguments that for the most part are 20 years old'. One might respond that we get bored too quickly, and that the demand for perpetual newness does not allow room for productive lingering and burrowing into certain refrains and pursuits. Those practices that have continued to pursue digital techniques as an explicit focus of their experimentation – such as Marc Fornes, biothing, kokkugia and supermanoeuvre (a few of the finer examples) – seem to be on a pathway towards increased fidelity: greater refinement, more sophisticated techniques, increased intricacy, and so on. The further they go, the more grotesquely or elegantly organic things appear, like intensified art nouveau taken across multiple levels of formal, structural and ornamental detail. This might not be disruptive, or transformative, innovation, but it is, in business speak, incremental innovation; the significant improvement or development of existing processes or products.[1]

However, Carpo has a more specific critique, arguing that the digital innovation occurring in other domains, successfully building on the participatory opportunities of Web 2.0, has not been approached in the experimentation of architects. He alludes to that which has become the architectural equivalent, where 'digital form finding invites a drastic redefinition of agency, not dissimilar from that which characterises the Web 2.0 at large'. Through some sleight of hand that turns digital form finding into an engagement with 'nature', designers 'become the midwives of emerging natural powers'. It is not entirely clear whether Carpo believes this midwifery is actually happening, or whether this is simply what some designers (naively) believe to

be happening. However, it is very clear that he is suspicious of it.

Whether one agrees with Carpo and his assessment of 'form finding' or not, if we approach the issue of the participatory, it does seem true that work which pursues computation as the primary media for designing is not often demonstrably strong in connecting with activity beyond the digital design space. In other words, the lid on the jar of digital form finding in architecture has, at times, become a little tight. As such, if there is any loss of 'innovative edge', one could understand this in terms of a loss of vitality, where states of disconnection, such as one sees in states of alienation and depression, can diminish potential for transformation and renewal (or innovation). Across all those eminently squirmy, organic, complex and intricate forms, there is a tendency to represent or mimic the vitality of the living, rather than to initiate or enact it. That said, even the most hermetic of formalism has value well beyond itself, in the manner through which it resonates with other similarly configured assemblages across socio-cultural activity. These formal assemblages feel 'contemporary' when they 'diagram' configurations of relations that are otherwise more sensed than seen – where, for instance, fields of similar but uniquely differentiated units (a hallmark of parametricism) resonate with cultural assumptions about identity. In this sense 'digital formalism' presents us with a certain vitality and sense of contemporary relevance in a way that moves beyond the mimicry that claims association with biological life.

While this diagrammatic resonance has value, two architectural practices have been breaking open digital hermeticism. The first is MOS (Michael Meredith and Hilary Sample), originally formed around 2003 under the name !@#? in New York. The second is New Territories, which encompasses R&Sie(n) and the newer formation [eIf/bʌt/c]. R&Sie(n) was

MOS (Michael Meredith and Hilary Sample)
with Tobias Putrih, *Temporary Cinema*,
Wexner Center for the Arts, Columbus,
Ohio, 2010
Wrapped around a column in Peter Eisenman's
Wexner Center gallery, this structure housed
a small cinema space in which gallery visitors
could sit and watch movies.

New Territories/R&Sie(n) with Benoit
Durandin, *Hypnochamber*, 'I've heard
about', Musée d'Art Moderne, Paris, 2005
This prototype/installation was staged as a
space for hypnosis, where one enters a 'wake up
dream' or fictional environment accessible only
via hypnosis.

founded in France in 1993 by François Roche with Stéphanie Lavaux and Gilles Deseveday. More recently, [eIf/bʌt/c], based in Bangkok, was formed (2011) by Roche with Camille Lacadée. Both MOS and New Territories/R&Sie(n) have developed upon major trajectories of computational design in ways that revitalise this discursive field by successfully reconnecting this kind of endeavour to broader cultural and social issues. In each case, one can certainly argue for disruptive rather than incremental innovation – becoming examples of how digital design in architecture is indeed reinventing itself.

A key tactic of both practices lies in operating across, with and through multiple media and dimensions of attention, situating themselves inside the very issues they are transforming. Actively working across writing and publishing, filmmaking, scripting and drawing, installations and buildings, they produce architecture that cannot be closed down, by any stretch of the imagination, to 'mere formalism'. Rather, there is a very evident striving to elicit transformations of what architecture is and can do. Each demonstrates, in different ways, how the closed computational design space can be blown open to produce architectures that are even stranger than the weirdest formalism. This gives the work a 'strange vitality'. The 'strangeness' being referred to is partly about quirky eccentricities, which is evident in both cases, but largely about the way in which their work implicates bodies (bodies encountering their work and the cultural fields in which those bodies operate) while escaping the anthropocentrism of the phenomenological tradition (their work is not focused on serving human sensation, feeling and experiential qualities). We become affected and implicated as they adeptly, and with cunning, loop us into that which the work is doing.

What is innovative, in other words, is not simply some aspect of the buildings or artefacts per se – although they each make significantly inventive, imaginative moves across their projects – but the way in which their work shifts the field of play through affecting bodies, architecture and cultural scenes via tactics that are not instrumental, but rather open and generative. Referring back to 'The Ethics of the Imperative' essay on pp 18–23 of this issue, these architectures implicates bodies and cultural milieus in ways that are akin to the virtuosity of Barbarella in the 'excessive machine'.

What is meant by the above can be explored through focusing largely on two installation projects: *Temporary Cinema* by MOS, with artist Tobias Putrih, at the Wexner Center for the Arts in Columbus, Ohio, in 2010, and *Hypnosis Chamber* (or *Hypnochamber*) by New Territories/R&Sie(n) with Benoit Durandin, which was part of the research project and exhibition 'I've heard about' at the Musée d'Art Moderne, Paris, in 2005. These installations have a number of immediate characteristics in common: both negotiate the existing structural elements of the galleries in which they are exhibited; both are porous, honeycomb or 3-D matrix structures; both exhibit certain properties of blur or fuzz; and both are made to elicit attention to other worlds – conjured through movies in the first instance, and hypnosis in the second.

In the website text for *Temporary Cinema*, MOS use their characteristically casual, or informal, mode of writing to describe it:

A collection of fuzzy structural lumps that glow and flicker with movies. Inside the fuzzy heap you can usually see people sitting, looking and listening. There isn't much to

MOS with Tobias Putrih, *Temporary Cinema*, Wexner Center for the Arts, Columbus, Ohio, 2010
Explicitly situating architecture in the relations between architectural artefacts and the narratives constructed around them, the project embodies a certain poignant relation to the way in which MOS uses film as an integral part of their architecture.

The installation offers the opportunity of lingering inside a 'parametric' environment to experience a double inhabitation – of both a built environment and filmic scenes and narratives. Described by MOS as a 'fuzzy heap' and an 'architectural mutt', the structure offers a certain rawness, or unfinished quality, through its sprayed, fuzzy surface treatment, recalling a metal structure sprayed with fire retardant commonly seen on building sites. This sense of incompletion is suggestive of their position that architecture is not simply about built structures per se, which are only part of the equation that counts as 'architecture'.

say, I guess it's parametric, it's constructed of voronoi cells in a video game physics environment, it's larger than it looks in photographs, it's not an abstract pristine grid, it's not floating. It's deformed through physics engines but doesn't quite touch settled on the ground. It's an architectural mutt, dishevelled but happy.'[2]

Picking up first on one aspect of the description ('I guess it's parametric, it's constructed of voronoi cells in a video game physics environment'): in this voronoi arrangement (a contagious favourite among digital designers for a time) that has been composed through the use of digital simulation (one might call this 'form finding'), we can see a direct association with the hallmark of parametric formalism: ie fields of similar but differentiated repeated units. However, as Meredith has made clear elsewhere, for example in his essay 'Never enough (transform, repeat ad nausea)',[3] the parametric form is simply not satisfying enough, and the architectural profession has tended to utilise parametrics in ways that 'fall short of its rich potential to correlate multivalent processes or typological transformations, parallel meanings, complex functional requirements, site-specific problems or collaborative networks'.[4]

Temporary Cinema addresses this shortfall through a few simple moves that work with and against the parametric. The first is by giving the installation a programme: a space to watch movies (formalist parametricism tends to avoid ambitions beyond the sculptural). This is not just any programme, however, because it requires that people linger inside this parametric environment to sit, look and listen – to be transported into filmic scenes and narratives such that they experience a double inhabitation. As John McMorrough has pointed out in an

essay specifically about the array of movies made by MOS: 'Architecture and cinema (or film, movies, television, videos) are both about inhabitation.'[5] MOS explicitly situate architecture in the space between object and text or narrative;[6] in other words, architecture is not buildings per se, but something that exists in the relations between architectural artefacts and the narratives constructed around them. This becomes especially clear in films they have made such as *Ordos* (2008) where an architectural model of a house, clearly another parametric form, moves through the changing light of day through night, overlaid with a text narrative about the interior lives of inhabitants X and Y. What we can or might understand about this architectural model is transformed by the text. The architecture is in the relation between this exterior view/model and interiorised relationships.

Temporary Cinema physically enacts the very conditions that, for MOS, constitute architecture, offering the inhabitation of two places at once (the built structure and narrative/film) – or, more precisely, the relations between them. This installation would have reached its full potential and poignancy had a film by MOS been screened in the *Temporary Cinema*, particularly one that involved this particular parametric construction. One can imagine something like their film *Escape (Correspondence)* (2009), which situates their Afterparty pavilion outside MoMA/PS1 in Queens, New York (2009) in a future narrative constructed as an anthropological analysis and speculation about the pavilion and its strange inhabitants. Actually, *Temporary Cinema* was used to screen a film series curated by the Wexner Center. However, the poignancy of MOS designing a cinema cannot be missed, given their overt interest in film. What becomes manifest here is the inhabitation of what they count as 'architecture', positioning people into a double inhabitation of the installation and film

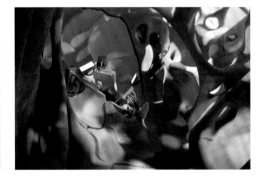

narrative such that their experience of both simultaneously becomes the architecture. As such, MOS installs us inside an architectural field they actively critique and transform.

The rub that one confronts here is that architecture, if it ever did have this, entirely loses any clear medium specificity. It is not about employing digital technologies or other representational media to generate or construct form; it is not about the use of physical substance in the production of built form; it is not about an architecture of text or narrative; and it is not simply about serving bodily experience either. It is all of these things – this is transversal architecture. However, this does not lead to a loss of medium specificity, but to a relocation of how we can understand the medium specificity of architecture into what we can summarise as 'affect': changes in the relations that condition environments in which we operate. Affect, quite simply, can be understood as what happens when things are poised on the edge of change, or in the process of changing. In conditions of change, there is risk and anticipation (what will happen next?), maybe nerves, stomach butterflies and twitches, changes in heartbeat, or flutters of joy, convulsions of laughter, and so on. These kinds of states are often understood as 'affects', but affect itself is the shifting of relations that can lead to an affective charge, or to these physical states or 'feelings'. If we understand affect in this way, innovation is always affective, and the more powerful or disruptive innovations are also more intensively affectively charged – giving rise to the sense of vitality. The approaches to architecture discussed here are subtly disruptive, making them all the more able to creep through the cracks and lodge themselves in the very sites they seek to disrupt and transform.

In the architecture of New Territories/R&Sie(n), working with affect is even more overt, and has explicit political agendas.

Their *Hypnochamber* project proposes to literally alter the state of the person inhabiting this structure:

> The hypno-chamber is produced as an indoor chamber, an immersion zone, where an hypnosis session has been registered and help citizens to escape from their alienated social condition.[7]

Hypnochamber does not situate itself in relation to parametricism or even computation as explicitly, or as self-consciously, as *Temporary Cinema*, but is clearly interested in this vocabulary. The larger project, 'I've heard about', that it is part of, presents a provocative, fictional scenario of an urban setting whose 'form no longer depends on the arbitrary decisions or control over its emergence exercised by a few, but rather the ensemble of its individual contingencies. It simultaneously subsumes premises, consequences and the ensemble of induced perturbations, in a ceaseless interaction.'[8] Rather than parametricism, 'I've heard about' picks up on the power of agent-based simulations that can model potential outcomes of the growth of an urban fabric that 'is based on negotiations between neighbours and other residents, and at the same time subject to collective constraints (accessibility and structural contradictions)'.[9] A 1:1 model of the larger scheme becomes the *Hypnochamber*, which offers a way to enter more deeply into this 1:1 fictional reality through hypnosis, with the provision of a place for the body to settle into the structure, surrounded by screens – a set-up for entering hypnosis. The project invites us, in other words, to enter into a strange loop wherein bodies become located deeply inside a space of indecipherable distinction between the 'real' and 'fiction'.

Perhaps, after all, through practices
like MOS and New Territories/R&Sie(n),
there is reason to be excited about
new trajectories emerging through and
out of digital design, and the capacity
of this area of design investigation to
reinvent itself.

Like MOS, New Territories/R&Sie(n) do not locate
'architecture' in the buildings they produce because
'construction is a byproduct, not a final term of the system or
scenario'.[10] Rather, architecture itself is more an assemblage,
a system of multiple concerns and dimensions. One of those
dimensions is text, or writing. The way in which *Hypnochamber*
aims to implicate bodies into its transformative agenda finds a
useful correlate in François Roche's recent project 'inklings' that
formed part of his guest-edited edition of New York journal
Log.[11] Printed on the postcard that always accompanies *Log*
(which typically spends its life inside the pages of the issue
as a bookmark) is an image of Roche's back in the process of
being tattooed. As part of the act of producing a journal issue,
Roche undertook to have text tattooed into his skin, and then
blocked out, to become a pattern of lines. He allows his body
to become like a subject of Franz Kafka's writing machine,
from the story 'In the Penal Colony' (first published in October
1919), which carves the sentence of condemned prisoners into
their skin before they die. However, like Barbarella (see pp
19–21), Roche survives the machine and the pain it inflicts,
precisely by accepting the forces at play inside a system, or
machine. Constantly playing with and making explicit notions
of protocol, contracts, domination and submission, Roche
approaches architectural practice as a matter of affecting and
being affected, from the inside: 'You infiltrate a situation and
are infiltrated. You have to accept a porosity.'[12]

The 'porosity' that Roche discusses is related to the way
in which theorist Robert Mitchell has discussed the affective
charge of the relatively new territory of biological art, or bioart.
In his book *Bioart and the Vitality of Media*,[13] he explores how
the idea of 'media', and in particular 'new media', might be

reviewed in light of these artistic practices. Surveying the field
and the basic contestations regarding what defines it, Mitchell
identifies 'vitalist bioart' as a way of distinguishing a particular
kind of bioart practice, linking it to a scientific tradition he
describes as 'experimental vitalism'. He locates vitalist bioart
in an 'experimentally generative' framework, rather than as a
primarily critical, ideological or analytical framework, even
though the latter are not excluded but rather folded into the
former. Mitchell tries to show that vitalist bioart works with
technologies and processes that render living material – including
you and me as biological entities – as the medium of the artistic
activity. In becoming a medium, our bodies are implicated in a
way that draws attention to their malleable plasticity, and their
plastic relations with other bodies. By plucking at a feeling of
changeability – ie ours, and of life beyond us – what Mitchell is
pointing to is less about bodies per se than affect as the medium.
In this sense, what he elucidates about what vitalist bioart is
doing is not dissimilar to that which MOS and New Territories/
R&Sie(n) do across their work. The feeling generated is aptly
described by Mitchell as a 'strange vitality', a lived quality of the
event in which we become implicated:

> Vitalist bioart is an attempt to amplify and modulate the
> affective experience of strange vitality, but as such, it also
> highlights 'wild type' experiences of the strange vitality that
> often attends the introduction of new media technologies....
> Moreover, by emphasizing the strange vitality of affective
> experiences of media, vitalist bioart points us toward a
> *generative* sense of media – that is, a sense of medium that
> moves beyond concepts of storage and communication and
> toward concepts of emergence.[14]

Log 25 postcard, 'inklings', François Roche, 2012
Every issue of New York journal *Log* is accompanied by a postcard. For Roche's guest-edited issue, the postcard image was of Roche's back in the process of being tattooed. As part of the act of producing a journal issue, Roche undertook to have text tattooed into his skin, and then blocked out, to become a pattern of lines. Through this affectively charged act, the changing/altering body becomes explicitly situated inside this text-based architectural event.

In moving towards emergence, this is a medium that engages an open, generative and ethically complex field because where these affects might go, and their unfolding implications, are not being dictated, nor is there an attempt to control something that will resist being controlled. This touches on the point that Oron Catts and Ionat Zurr make in their essay in this issue (pp 70–75): ie, when dealing with the complexity of biological life, it is dangerously naive to hope for the control an engineer – or an engineering mindset – might expect. If vitalist bioart, as well as the work of MOS and New Territories/R&Sie(n), trigger a feeling of 'strange vitality', this feeling is also very much hanging on the edge of what might emerge. However, this is not because there is a lack of intention, but that the intention is part of that engagement within those relations – and is directed at, for instance, what is generated between buildings and the narratives around them, or within fields of shifting relations. There is both critique and a striving to transform in certain directions, without the attempts of the do-gooder, the positive instrumentalist, the dictator, etc, to control things outside of themselves.

Perhaps, after all, through practices like MOS and New Territories/R&Sie(n), there is reason to be excited about new trajectories emerging through and out of digital design, and the capacity of this of design investigation to reinvent itself. If we have grown tired of the metaphorical, biomimetic and other loose associations with the 'organic' or biological that digital design so frequently adopts, maybe the point of contact lies intertwined in the realm of affect as the new medium of our post-9/11 era. ⌂

Notes
1. Tony Wagner, *Creating Innovators: The Making of Young People Who Will Change the World*, Scribner (New York), 2012, pp 9–10.
2. www.mos-office.net.
3. Michael Meredith, 'Never enough (transform, repeat ad nausea)', in Tomoko Sakamoto, Albert Fere and Michael Kubo (eds), *From Control to Design: Parametric/Algorithmic Architecture*, Actar (Barcelona), 2008, pp 6–9.
4. Ibid, p 6.
5. John McMorrough, 'MOS Movies, or the Phantasmagoria Of Discipline', *Log* 24, Winter/Spring 2012, p 111.
6. Symposium and panel discussion, 'The Eclipse of Beauty: Parametric Beauty' (Mario Carpo, Michael Meredith and Ingeborg Rocker), Harvard University, September 2011: www.gsd.harvard.edu/#/media/the-eclipse-of-beauty-parametric-beauty-mario-carpo-michael.html.
7. www.new-territories.com/hypnosisroom.htm.
8. Ibid.
9. http://b.durandin.free.fr/iveheardabout/iha.htm.
10. From Pia Ednie-Brown's interview with François Roche, April 2012.
11. François Roche, *Log 25: Reclaim Resi(lience)stance*, Summer 2012.
12. From Pia Ednie-Brown's interview with François Roche, April 2012.
13. Robert Mitchell, *Bioart and the Vitality of Media*, University of Washington Press (Seattle, WA), 2010.
14. Ibid, p 92.

Artists and researchers **Oron Catts and Ionat Zurr** of SymbioticA, based at the School of Anatomy, Physiology and Human Biology at the University of Western Australia, are internationally renowned as pioneers in the field of biological arts, challenging audiences with their tissue engineering projects. Catts and Zurr discuss how synthetic biology has increasingly become 'the new frontier for exploitation' and why there is currently 'a resurgence of the application of engineering logic in the fields of the life sciences' in which life itself becomes a raw material.

THE VITALITY OF MATTER AND THE INSTRUMEN- TALISATION OF LIFE

Oron Catts and Ionat Zurr, *Disembodied Cuisine*, Tissue Culture & Art Project, SymbioticA, School of Anatomy, Physiology and Human Biology, University of Western Australia, 2003
The first time a semi-living frog steak (or in-vitro frog meat) was grown and consumed in a nouvelle-cuisine-style meal.

An interesting phenomenon is emerging, heralded by developments in the life sciences and applied technologies, coupled with the introduction of engineering principles – specifically in the field of synthetic biology. The further life is being instrumentalised, becoming a product for human manipulation, matter – whether living, semi-living or non-living – is being attributed with vitality and agency. Some refer to this as a 'new materialism', most notably Gilles Deleuze, Manuel De Landa and Jane Bennett.[1] It is what we refer to as 'secular vitalism'. More than anything this phenomenon further blurs the perceptual (and technological) boundaries between what we consider living, semi-living and non-living.

The 1993 publication in *Science* of the paper 'Tissue Engineering' by Robert Langer and Joseph P Vacanti represented a major departure from the ways in which bodies had previously been considered, treated and fixed.[2] It promised to find ways to unlock the latent abilities of the body to regenerate by combining principles of biology and engineering. The body was not just to become a regenerative site, embedded within this proposition of combining biology and engineering; there is an entirely new capacity to engineer functional biological systems outside of the body with a wide range of applications.

The image that became associated with the promise of tissue engineering – the BBC's 'Tomorrow's World' footage reels of a nude mouse with a human ear sprouting from its back (1995) – demonstrated nicely the surreal outcome of attempting to combine two contradictory mindsets: the messiness of life and the cold hard logic of rational design and the engineering approach. Nevertheless, the idea of growing functional tissue 'products' has been extremely seductive.

Life is increasingly seen as the new frontier for exploitation;

from industrial farming through in-vitro meat and bio-prospecting to synthetic biology, life is extracted from its natural context into the realm of the manufactured. Though there is nothing new about this, in recent years we have witnessed a resurgence of the application of engineering logic in the fields of the life sciences, along with the treatment of life as a raw material for anthropocentric uses. As observed by Evelyn Fox Keller in 2009: 'The engineering standpoint houses multiple aims: two in particular stand out here: creation and efficiency.'[3] When the two principles of human creation coupled with the capitalist notion of efficiency are employed on living matter there is a promise of both top-down and bottom-up systems of control.

The application of engineering logic to life has historical precedents. Already in 1895, HG Wells reflected on the body as a malleable entity in his essay 'The Limits of Individual Plasticity', saying: 'The generalisation of heredity may be pushed to extreme, to an almost fanatical fatalism.'[4] A year later Wells demonstrated some of these ideas and their possible consequences in his novel *The Island of Doctor Moreau*. The plasticity of life's processes, through human intervention not in the fictional realm, was demonstrated quite spectacularly only three years later in 1899 when Jacob Loeb developed what he called 'artificial parthenogenesis … the artificial production of normal larvae (plutei) from the unfertilized eggs of the sea urchin'.[5] In other words, Loeb demonstrated the capacity for fertilisation (in a sea urchin) without the use of sperm. Following his discovery, he wrote: 'It is in the end still possible that I find my dream realized, to see a constructive or engineering biology in place of a biology that is merely analytical.'[6]

In 1890 Loeb wrote: 'The idea is now hovering before me that man himself can act as a creator, even in living Nature,

forming it eventually according to his will. Man can at least succeed in a technology of living substance.'[7] Like many of the engineers working with biology today, Loeb promoted the idea of science as manipulation in favour of what was practised then – science of observation. The hands-on, experiential engagement with materials is also a characteristic of some contemporary artistic engagements with the life sciences such as the works researched at SymbioticA, School of Anatomy, Physiology and Human Biology, University of Western Australia.[8] However, there are some fundamental differences: instead of efficiency and utility, some of the artistic engagement is purposely about futility and cultural discussions, reflections and observations. The position of the designer within this area is still to be scrutinised.

Biologists know that in order to achieve some level – if very limited – of control in living systems, they have to be isolated and reduced as much as possible to the point that the components of these biological systems cannot function and be understood in their original context. In other words, life is context dependent, and living materials will therefore act and respond through its milieu – in that sense the material is vital.

Crude Matter, an ongoing artistic project, is concerned with the importance of the substrate – the context – for life; the context is vital to life development and differentiation as much as, if not more than, the genetic code. Lately there has been a growing realisation that this differentiation depends very much on the extracellular matrixes on which stem cells are growing; even a subtle change in substrate morphology will have a fundamental effect on the cells' plasticity and the lineage they will take.

In the paper 'Substrate Stiffness Affects Early Differentiation Events in Embryonic Stem Cells', Nicholas D Evens et al demonstrate how the mere changes in the stiffness of the substrate Polydimethylsiloxane (PDMS) will change the path of differentiation of stem cells into different types of tissue such as bone and fat.[9] Loosely based on the story of the Golem (literally meaning 'crude' and 'unshaped'), Crude Matter explores the 'alchemy like' transformation of materials into active substrates that have the ability to act as surrogates and upon life. The story of the Golem describes the emergence of life from inanimate matter (mud); life that is forceful and visceral and can be shaped for different purposes and intentions. The purpose of Crude Matter is a poetic exploration that brings to the fore the materiality of life in context. This is different to the hegemony of the metaphor of life as a code. Drawing on medieval references, the aim is to look at engineered life that is on the edges of what we now consider the animate or inanimate – and to provide it with some sort of agency, even if it is symbolic.

In 2010, the American biologist and entrepreneur Craig Venter declared that he had created the first life form with a 'parent as a computer'.[10] He was referring here to Ventner's engineered bacterial cell, the *Mycoplasma laboratorium* (aka 'Synthia') where his group sequenced the genome of *Mycoplasma genitalium* and transferred it into a bacteria cell from which the original DNA was removed. Even though what Venter achieved is indeed a great technological feat – being able to synthesise the longest chain of DNA and replace a genome of a simple bacteria with a synthesised version – the context (that is, the cell and its contents) is still of biological origin. The role of the computer in synthesising the genome was actually only that of a glorified copier – copying a genome without fully 'understanding' its meaning. The only novel part that was introduced to the genome was a 'watermark' – a hidden message

This blue-lit cabinet is situated at the far end of the display. It contains the only living element in the work: hybridomas cells in the WAVE bioreactor (a surrogate, technological body). These life forms are abstracted from their source, yet are living and growing. It may be time to find a place in our ecology for 'neolife'.

An updated cabinet of curiosities: the two-headed bird recalls the fascination with oddities and their significance in the 17th century. Museums have conventions in displaying preserved life forms, and this display questions ideas about a progressive complexity of species.

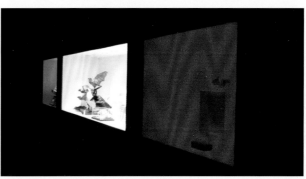

that contained the names of the researchers, a URL and quotes relating to creation of life – something that the artist Joe Davis had done back in the mid-1980s showing once again that artists can precede scientists in conceptual breakthroughs.[11]

Back in 1996, we coined the term 'semi-living' to describe tissue constructs that are grown/constructed and exist outside of 'natural' bodies in techno-scientific ones (a Petri dish or bioreactor). The term was chosen for this new class of object/ being that continues to populate our environment in its different and varied forms and utilities for descriptive as well as poetic reasons: the former being the cell constructs that have living aspects but are dependent on technological support and are not 'fully' living, and are poetic. They are liminal beings that are part of us – but different to us. Though controlled by us in some respects, they can (and do) 'escape' our intentions. Their agency is always in question.

Another project currently being researched, *Tissue Engineered Muscle Actuators as Evocative Cultural Objects and Vehicles for Discourses about Material Agency and Living Things*, concerns the development of an artistic electro-mechanical device that will facilitate growth and formation of muscle fibres, thus enabling the conditions (such as temperature, sterility, nutrient media, morphological and biomechanical elements) necessary to maintain life and encourage growth.[12] These specific cells have the potential to mechanically and chemically contract and expand if grown in specific conditions. The device thus has the primary function of organising and amplifying the inherent movement behaviour of the muscle fibres, thus giving the cells the potential to become a moving semi-living machine. The use of muscle tissue as semi-living labour further problematises the distinction between the living (whether human or other animal) and the machine (whether living – ie woman, slave or animal – or non-living), and emphasises some absurdities concerned with ideal notions of technological solutions and technological efficiencies.

The *Tissue Engineered Muscle Actuators* project embodies this paradox; on the one hand it can be seen as a straightforward example of the instrumentalisation of life, using tissue to create a living machine, an actuator. However, it is hoped that it will have more subtle yet important affects and effects; through the inherent movement of the tissue-engineered muscle, the intention is to create a more visceral 'embodied empathy' with the living twitching machine, one that will make us feel uneasy.

The tension between engineering's futile attempts to control and measure the force and displacement of the myotubes, developing skeletal muscle fibres with a tubular appearance that are absurdly small in scale, and the incredible complexity of the myotubes as matter, is a point of interest. By amplifying the movement of the semi-living muscle myotubes, we seek, in a visceral sense, to examine its agency.

Thus, from a conceptual and scholarly point of view, the tensions surrounding bare life machine dependency and movement as a life sign can be combined to generate discourses of new relations and empathies with different gradients of life, for a more visceral understanding of the human position within its environment. Through the attribution, even if symbolic, of agency to the different gradients of animate and inanimate (also hybrid) entities, and the understanding of how such elements carry their vital force through relationships of effect and affect, fragments of life may be revitalised and re-contextualised.[13]

Is it part of us, as living beings, to show affinity to life that is drastically different to non-living matter? It may be argued

Oron Catts and Ionat Zurr, *The Semi-Living Worry Dolls*, Tissue Culture & Art Project, SymbioticA, School of Anatomy, Physiology and Human Biology, University of Western Australia, 2012
In this exhibit, audiences were encouraged to whisper into a designated microphone and express their worries to growing semi-living dolls, each in a microgravity rotary cell culture. A speaker positioned near the dolls played them the recorded worries of the audience.

Back in 1996, we coined the term 'semi-living' to describe tissue constructs that are grown/constructed and exist outside of 'natural' bodies in techno-scientific ones (a Petri dish or bioreactor).

Ionat Zurr, Oron Catts and Chris Salter, *Untitled*, Tissue Culture & Art Project, SymbioticA, School of Anatomy, Physiology and Human Biology, University of Western Australia, 2012
left: A collection of C2C12 skeletal muscle cells grown and differentiated to form myotubes. Myotubes are a fusion of myoblasts into multi-nuclei cells. Myoblasts eventually develop to a mature muscle fibre. The myotubes were grown as part of the research into Tissue Engineered Muscle Actuators as evocative cultural objects and vehicles for discourses about material agency and living machines.

right: A single C2C12 skeletal muscle cell, or myoblast, originated from mice, photographed under an inverted microscope with x20 magnification.

that stepping on a cockroach is less unsettling than dropping one's laptop. But still, let us insist, beyond the consequences of the incident for you, there may be a fundamental difference between taking life away and a mechanical shutdown. As a society, can we show and practise care for life (whatever shape, complexity or constitution it may evolve into) that does not resort to non-materialist vitalism (such as a higher or purpose-driven force)? Although the initial idea of the semi-livings came from a design perspective, we pursued it as artists in the belief that this position will enable us to question, critique and problematise the instrumentalisation and objectification of the semi-livings being created. As artists, we hope that we have a different 'contract' with society – we ought to provoke, question and reveal hypocrisies through different tactics: whether aesthetic, absurd/ironic or subtle confrontation. Making our audience uneasy is an outcome of our own uneasiness, perusing the very things that make us uncomfortable. All we propose to offer are contestable future scenarios that are different from the canon of the contemporary trajectories. ∆

Notes
1. For more see: Gilles Deleuze and Félix Guattari, *A Thousand Plateaus*, University of Minnesota Press (Minneapolis, MN), 1993; Manuel De Landa, *A Thousand Years of Nonlinear History*, Zone Books (New York), 1997; and Jane Bennett, *Vibrant Matter: A Political Ecology of Things*, Duke University Press (Durham, NC and London), 2010.
2. Robert Langer and Joseph P Vacanti, 'Tissue Engineering', *Science*, Vol 260, No 5110, May 1993, pp 920–6.
3. Evelyn Fox Keller, 'What Does Synthetic Biology Have to Do with Biology?', *BioSocieties*, Vol 4, Issue 2–3, September 2009, p 291.
4. HG Wells, 'The Limits of Individual Plasticity', in Robert Philmus and David Y Hughes (eds), *HG Wells: Early Writing in Science and Science Fiction*, University of California Press (Berkeley, CA), 1975, p 36.
5. Jacques Loeb, 'On the Nature of the Process of Fertilization and the Artificial Production of Normal Larvae (Plutei) from the Unfertilized Eggs of the Sea Urchin', *American Journal of Physiology* 3, 1899, pp 135–8; reprinted in *Studies in General Physiology*, University of Chicago Press (Chicago, IL), 1905, pp 539–43.
6. Jacques Loeb to Ernst Mach, 28 December 1899. Cited in Philip J Pauly, *Controlling Life: Jacques Loeb and the Engineering Ideal in Biology*, Oxford University Press (New York), 1987, p 93.
7. Ibid, p 4.
8. www.symbiotica.uwa.edu.au/.
9. Nicholas D Evans, Caterina Minelli, Eileen Gentleman, Vanessa LaPointe, Sameer N Patankar, Maria Kallivretaki, Xinyong Chen, Clive J Roberts and Molly M Stevens, *European Cells and Materials*, Vol 18, 2009, pp 1–14.
10. www.ted.com/talks/craig_venter_unveils_synthetic_life.html.
11. Joe Davis, 'Microvenus', *Art Journal* 55 (1), 1996, pp 70–4.
12. The project is in collaboration with Professor Miranda Grounds, Dr Stuart Hodgetts and Professor Chris Salter.
13. For more see: Andrew Pickering, *The Mangle of Practice: Time, Agency, and Science*, University of Chicago Press (Chicago, IL), 1995, and Jane Bennett, op cit.

Oron Catts and Ionat Zurr, *Victimless Leather: A Prototype of Stitch-less Jacket grown in a Technoscientific 'Body'*, Tissue Culture & Art Project, SymbioticA, School of Anatomy, Physiology and Human Biology, University of Western Australia, 2012
The artists use a range of media including a custom-made perfusion pump, biodegradable polymer, nutrient media and living cells. The piece was presented as part of the 'Crude Life: The Tissue Culture & Art Project Retrospective' in Gdansk, Poland, in 2012.

Oron Catts and Ionat Zurr, *Victimless Leather: A Prototype of Stitch-less Jacket grown in a Technoscientific 'Body'*, Tissue Culture & Art Project, SymbioticA, School of Anatomy, Physiology and Human Biology, University of Western Australia, 2010
Exhibited as part of the 'Medicine and Art: Imagining a Future for Life and Love' exhibition at the Mori Art Museum, Tokyo, this jacket-like construct is grown out of an immortal cell line. The image depicts a fungal contamination of the cell construction.

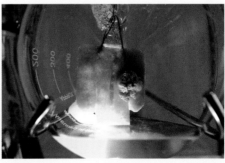

INITI
CHANG
ARCHITECTING THE
WITH ARAKAWA AND

ATING
E
BODY-ENVIRONMENT
GINS

Arakawa and Gins, *Study for a baseball field for the architectural body*, 1992
These artists-turned-architects produced many terrain studies that emphasise the
degree to which actions change with shifts in topography.

New York-based artists Shusaku Arakawa (1936–2010) and Madeline Gins (1941–) used architecture in their work in an approach that they have referred to as 'architecting'. **Jondi Keane** explains how as artists-turned-architects, 'Arakawa and Gins have not been particularly interested in innovating architecture, but in approaching architecture as a way to innovate, or change the world'.

The written, built and unbuilt works of Arakawa and Gins represent the outside of architecture. As artists-turned-architects, they are primarily concerned with enacting body-environments rather than producing environments for bodies to inhabit. This means that they do not consider architecture as a standalone entity, but as something inseparable from our bodies, and how and what we can become. More concisely, their concern is architecting rather than architecture.[1] To some extent, they founded the New York-based Architectural Body Research Foundation (1987) to foreground architecting as a way to ask questions, where those questions are posed in order to initiate change. While Marcel Duchamp put painting back in service of the mind, Arakawa and Gins put architecture in service of (changing) the body, which rings a dissonant, dissident chord in a profession where innovation often conserves value.

Arakawa and Gins have not been particularly interested in innovating architecture, but in approaching architecture as a way to innovate, or change the world. Architecture for them operates as an evolutionary trigger and architecting as an 'exaption'. Exaption (exaptation or pre-adaptation) refers to the way the features of an organism might be suited to, or co-opted by, a new function.[2] Whereas exaption does not imply any futuristic or anticipatory faculty in evolution, Arakawa and Gins' procedural architecture does propose that new combinations of sensing and new modes of perception, action and co-selection can be anticipated and prompted into existence.

There have been many commentators on Arakawa and Gins' projects who have unpacked the way they work on the context and conditions of meaning that shape the structure and appearance of the world.[3] This discussion will therefore emphasise the experimental and process-oriented nature of their work, that deals with the human organism from the point of view of the inseparable organism-environment. The ongoing nature of their practice is constantly signalled in their writing by the use of the present-participle verb form 'ing', which as Jean-Jacques Lecercle observes, marks the time of a process (becoming) and tentatively fixes the results of a process into the name of an entity: for example, 'architect-ing'.[4] Architecting as an ongoing provisional event and enduring set of results, in the hands of Arakawa and Gins, makes architecture into a tool for daily research. What float to the surface from the persistence of practice are questions about the values of, or beliefs about, the world, and the rules to which we cling.

The architecting of Arakawa and Gins reassembles the bridge between the know-how of making and the ready-made of thinking. On this bridge, perception is action, and one may research 'action in perception'.[5] Arakawa and Gins suggest we start with the shape of awareness evident in the habits of an 'organism that persons'.[6] These habits regulate what we know and how knowledge becomes know-how. Arakawa and Gins destabilise these habits by rendering visible the

Arakawa and Gins, Panel 3, Section 7, 'Splitting Meaning', *The Mechanism of Meaning*, 1963–73
The 82 panels organised into 15 subdivisions challenge viewers with puzzles and invite an exploration and interrogation of the various conceptual and perceptual processes that interfere or enhance our ability to perceive, therefore changing the way we construct meaning.

Arakawa and Gins, 'Gaze Brace' room, Bridge of Reversible Destiny, 1973–90
Originally designed to span the river in Epinal, France, the bridge makes the cognitive puzzles of *The Mechanism of Meaning* into an immersive environment that questions the habitual connections between sensory reception and bodily orientation. The 'Gaze Brace' room has a bird's-eye view within it, allowing a person to be in two places at once in the room. 1/20 scale model.

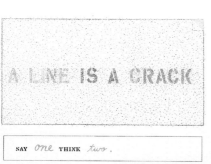

precariousness of identity boundaries and the apparently automatic functions of the body that hold them in place. From the outset of their collaboration in the 1960s they confronted audiences with choices between conceptual and perceptual information in the 'splitting of meaning', where a line is a crack and a conceptual demarcation. These experiments in the embodied nature of meaning destabilised the insular nature of the self and the habits of making sense. They were organised into tasks and sections that became known as *The Mechanism of Meaning*.[7]

The programme of 82 panel puzzles that made up *The Mechanism of Meaning* consists of two parts. The first part entails the dismantling of habitual processing that tended to ignore the role of perceiving and sensing in favour of linguistic and conceptual engagement. The second involves a reassembling process prompted by several approaches intended to transform the relationship between sensation and the logic of sense. The expansion of this project into immersive environments required that Arakawa and Gins shift from confrontations confined to the page or the painting, and consider a procedural approach. In doing so, architectural surrounds became the means by which to study 'which types of bodily movements … are most conducive to an optimal *tentative constructing towards a holding in place,* and which constructed discursive sequences best constrain them'.[8]

The built environments produced from this process –

the Bridge of Reversible Destiny/The Process in Question proposal (1989), Site of Reversible Destiny – Yoro Park, Gifu Prefecture, Japan (1995), Ubiquitous Site in the Nagi Museum of Contemporary Art, Katsuta, Japan (1994), and the Bioscleave House, Long Island, New York (2007) – dilate the space of engagement, questioning all of the exploratory movements, sensory modalities and conceptual measures at work (or at play) within a built surround. Most notably, the 'Gaze Brace' room on the Bridge of Reversible Destiny included a bird's-eye view of itself that exists as a built feature within the room. Once again a question is directly posed by an environment: In what ways would you, as an 'organism that persons', coordinate the variety of sensory information doubled by this room? The built view of the room from above can be understood as a plan perceived as a feature of the room, literally placing a person in two places at once. The ensuing responses to being situated in this way cross-reference the bird's-eye view with a current location. After recalibrating the way two embodied experiences interact, thinking and feeling are on more intimate terms.

So how would one prototype the architectural features of a built environment for the purposes of exaption? The architecting process of Arakawa and Gins aspires to build environments that provide the conditions by which existing modes of sensing might exapt; that is, find a new operational modality. Perhaps more interestingly, Arakawa and Gins' built

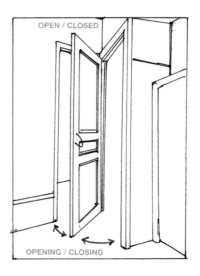

Jondi Keane, **Drawing of Marcel Duchamp's
Door, 11 rue Larrey,** 1927
Arakawa was a protégé of Duchamp, and
together with Madeline Gins continued to explore
paradoxes, ironies and 'infrathin' relationships
through architectural means. Where Duchamp's
Door explores the paradox of a door being
open and closed at the same time, Arakawa and
Gins explore the way we determine size, scale,
distance, surface and horizon in similarly elegant
built propositions.

*As a thought experiment it remains a paradox that pits two
identity states against each other. But as a built feature of
the world, the door, as something with which one interacts,
is always in the process of opening and closing.*

surrounds might initiate a change in the body-environment that
was not anticipated, but sits patiently adjacent to the current
state of affairs. This body-environment approach to the
emergence of meanings makes the linguistic prompts in *The
Mechanism of Meaning,* such as 'Say one, think two', and the
architectural prompt of 'Gaze Brace', into techniques for the
exaption of cognition.[9]

The value of Arakawa and Gins' work is their interest in the
link between selection and self-organisation. This is a matter
of both evolutionary importance and everyday significance.
It is wherein the viability of the human organism resides.
To discover how Arakawa and Gins arrived at exaption, a
detour back to their friend and protégé Marcel Duchamp is
necessary. It is Duchamp's experimentation with built paradox
that may be cited as the prototype of exaptive environments.
Duchamp's *Door, 11 rue Larrey* (1927) provides a physical
challenge to Aristotle's logic of identity, which excludes
a middle point between A and not-A to maintain logical
distinctions as 'either this or that' and never 'this and that'.
The door instantiates the excluded middle. It can be identified
as both open and closed because it is built into a corner with
two door jams. As a thought experiment it remains a paradox
that pits two identity states against each other. But as a built
feature of the world, the door, as something with which one
interacts, is always in the process of opening and closing. Its
actual position in the world turns against the logic of identity,

becoming ironic and demonstrative of what Duchamp called
the 'infrathin'.

The infrathin represents Duchamp's proposition that
there are imperceptible differences in seemingly identical
things, and this small distinction both separates things and
allows for the passage of one thing to another.[10] Positioning
the audience as arbiter of the opening and closing door,
it remains in a never-to-be-fully-determined state. At each
position, Duchamp's *Door* exists in two states despite its own
impossibility, which it continuously disproves provisionally.
Standing in relation to the door, one must choose the limits
and define the parameters of the world under construction.
At its most definitive state secure in one door jam, the door
is categorically both open and closed, otherwise its status is
always in a state of play. Enacting the opening and closing of
the door is an architecting activity best examined in-situ with
all body-environmental information in play. This proof, involving
the logic of identity, is a demonstration, a protest, or perhaps
a petition for the way material processes can be used to
question logic and how the questioning of logic can be used
to initiate change. Changing identity changes relations;
changing relations changes interaction, which in turn allows
agents to enact a world, newly configured.

Like Duchamp's *Door,* the architecting procedures of
Arakawa and Gins aim to initiate action only in order to initiate
change. And the difference between initiating action and

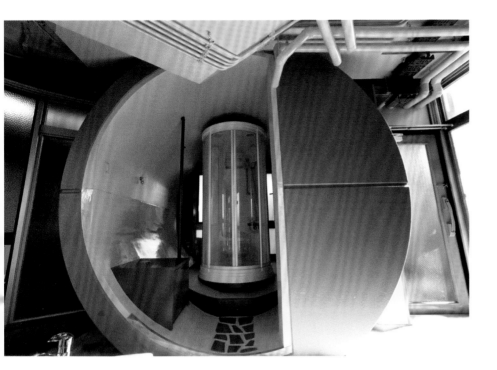

Arakawa and Gins, Bathroom,
Reversible Destiny Lofts, Mitaka,
Japan, 2006
The wedge entrance to the bathroom, like
Duchamp's *Door*, begs the question of
open or enclosed in a room that is a tube
intersected by a tubular shower. Here, the
characteristics that would determine the
identity of a given feature are challenged,
requiring exploratory movement rather than
recollected actions to navigate the built
environment.

initiating change is the difference between working inside
a system and working to change the conditions by which
meaning and value are designated. Where Duchamp's work
makes the perceiver understand the difficulty of choosing
persistence or change, logic or interpretation, Arakawa and
Gins relocate that set of choices from descriptions of the
world to the perceiver's operations of attention, selection,
decision and judgement.

Arakawa and Gins take Duchamp's prototype and place
it into a context where the problem that the excluded
middle poses is dispersed across the conditions of a built
environment where living becomes daily research. Like
Duchamp's *Door,* the entranceway to the bathroom in the
Reversible Destiny Lofts in Mitaka, Japan (2006) is open and
closed, enclosing and revealing, but without the movement
of a door. Instead, the designation of private and public
depends upon the movement of the resident researcher.
Negotiating the changing slope of the floor while managing to
squeeze around the cylindrical shower that bisects the room
requires that the decisions regarding enclosure or exposure
are linked to the proprioceptive, kinaesthetic and perceptual
determinations produced by moving through the room.

While initiating action amplifies the motivation for
relationships that already exist to be activated more quickly,
more intensely and with more valences, initiating change
shifts modes of sensing and scales of action across the

organism–person–surround. Arakawa and Gins offer a
practice (architecting) that observes and transforms habit into
exaption, and action into change. They accomplish this shift
through a range of tactics, two of which are worthy of note.
First, they situate the resident-researcher as the beneficiary of
the experimental findings, and second, as a result of acquiring
knowledge first-hand, the subject is equipped to continue the
process, potentially inventing and assembling new questions,
hypotheses and procedures to be investigated architecturally.

If Duchamp's *Door* highlights the infrathin to erode
the conditions of distinct identity, then Arakawa and Gins'
procedural architecture disperses the question of identity
across the modes of perception and action that construct
identity distinctions. Perhaps the way to understand how an
environment might prompt exaption is to find what activity
precedes the initiating of action, and thereby find a way to
operate on the automatic functions that pave the way to
purposeful action and conscious perception. Shaun Gallagher,
in *How the Body Shapes the Mind* (2005), coined the term
'prenoetic' to describe the way persons are already moving or
reaching for a cup before they think/intend/decide to reach
for it.[11] Intention is anticipated by the ongoing processing of
the conditions of body-environment readiness. Whether these
forms of readiness are ready-made or are ready-to-make
depends upon the qualities of the environment and the degree
to which it holds automatic functions in place.

Arakawa and Gins, Bioscleave House,
East Hampton, Long Island, New York,
2007
At every turn and step in the Bioscleave
House, the features by which to determine
size, distance, horizon, slope and time,
collapse. There is no unifying system
by which to set a measure or to refer
for correlation. As a result, a finer and
more varied interaction of the senses is
needed to ground one's sense of self and
to re-establish an orientation to the built
environment.

Arakawa and Gins' built environments make you aware, right away, of your position. In some ways they make you aware of your stance, whether or not you will engage with the invitations and prompting embodied in the work, and then what form the engagement will take.

Arakawa and Gins, Table study for the Reversible Destiny
Healing Fun House, Palm Springs, California, 2012
In the Bioscleave House, Reversible Destiny Loft and the proposal
for the Reversible Destiny Healing Fun House, plan views of the
built environment appear in order to provide multiple views of an
environment within itself to dilate awareness of body-environment
interactions and prompt new ways of sensing, thinking and feeling.

Arakawa and Gins offer a way to understand architectural innovation as a perpetual state by integrally involving the built environment in the act of striving to constantly reassemble how we join, separate and apportion the world. In short, they demonstrate how the built environment can play a critical role in initiating change. Daily research and architectural procedures make every aspect of every activity suspect, tentative and reconfigurable. The Bioscleave House, for example, enacts a 'disperse to contrast procedure' and 'tentative constructing towards a holding in place procedure'.[12] Architectural procedures provide a way to understand encounters in their built environment. Arakawa and Gins' essay 'Directions for Architectural Procedure Invention and Assembly'[13] suggests how procedures may become a research methodology to prompt the building of new (built) questions. Gins is continuing the duo's procedural work after the untimely death of Arakawa in 2010, inventing new procedures such as the 'scale-jugging procedure' in the Reversible Destiny Healing Fun House (a community centre in Palm Springs, California). The new projects re-examine the questions posed in the Bioscleave House and the Mitaka Reversible Destiny Lofts, focusing on the link between perceptual learning and the way volumes are constructed, textured and held in place.[14]

Bioscleave House and the Reversible Destiny Healing Fun House are exaptive environments. Their procedural approach

Arakawa and Gins, Reversible Destiny Healing Fun House, Palm Springs, California, 2012
The latest work of Arakawa and Gins, begun before Arakawa's death in 2010, utilises the characteristic undulating floor, the pitched ceiling (from the Bioscleave House, 2007), the open walls of multilevel labyrinth (from the Site of Reversible Destiny – Yoro Park, Gifu Prefecture, Japan, 1995) and the circular room (from the Reversible Destiny Lofts, Mitaka, 2006) to intensify awareness of volume and scale when engaging with the environment.

Enriched environments, physical cross-training, puzzle solving and a host of other exercises help with neural connections not only for rehabilitation, but for general health and longevity. Arakawa and Gins assert the importance of architecture as a tool that can anticipate or 'exapt' the potential of the perceptual system, focusing on ways the body and environment join and separate to achieve different goals.

makes an inhabitant ask: 'How big am I, how far from the door, the pole and the wall? What is level, how does vision help maintain balance? How does balance affect perceiving the pitch of the ceiling, and how does movement transform perception? Ultimately, am I able to move across modes of sensing and scales of action?'

Arakawa and Gins' built environments make you aware, right away, of your position. In some ways they make you aware of your stance, whether or not you will engage with the invitations and prompting embodied in the work, and then what form the engagement will take. Once the ways of making a distinction become tentative, the notion of body becomes moot, and questioning the body-environment becomes paramount. Arakawa and Gins' environments investigate the conditions most conducive to prompt the body's plasticity. They want to know what types of architecting actions would support changes in co-selection. The question that architecture becomes is how to get the setup right? How, or in what form, can a 360-degree question be asked? The questions must be built to be asked sufficiently. The answers to architectural questions will be multiple and variegated. Architecture that questions living is always against death, pressing the infinitive case ('to not to die') of possibility against the logic of identity. Arakawa and Gins' approach to innovation is long-term, aiming to dilate the ongoing newness of making – and the remaking of ourselves. Δ

Notes
1. Ed Keller comment to Johannes Knesl: 'I don't think that Eisenman wants us to absolutely invent ourselves.' From Ed Keller, Johannes Knesl, Greg Lynn and Jesse Reiser, 'Four Architects on *Reversible Destiny*', *Reversible Destiny: We Have Decided Not to Die*, compiled by Michael Govan, Guggenheim Museum (New York), 1997, p 217.
2. See Stephen Jay Gould and Elisabeth S Vrba, 'Exaptation: A Missing Term in the Science of Form', *Paleobiology* 8(1), 1982, pp 4–15.
3. A large group of scholars and practitioners across a wide range of enquiries have been attracted to and written about their work, including Hans-Georg Gadamer, Jean-François Lyotard, Italo Calvino, Arthur Danto, George Lakoff, Mark Taylor, Mark Hansen, Andrew Benjamin, Charles Bernstein, Shaun Gallagher, Jean-Jacques Lecercle, Hideo Kawamoto, Jean-Michel Rabaté, Dorothea Olkowski, Tom Conley, Erin Manning and Brian Massumi.
4. Jean-Jacques Lecercle, 'Ing', for AG3 Online: Third international Arakawa and Gins: Philosophy and Architecture Conference, 2010. See http://ag3.griffith.edu.au/.
5. Alva Noë, *Action in Perception*, MIT Press (Cambridge, MA and London), 2004.
6. Madeline Gins and Shusaku Arakawa, *Architectural Body*, University of Alabama Press (Tuscaloosa, AL), 2002, pp 2–4.
7. Arakawa and Gins, 'The Mechanism of Meaning', in *Reversible Destiny: We Have Decided Not to Die*, op cit, pp 54–111.
8. Gins and Arakawa, *Architectural Body*, op cit, p 59. See also the chapter 'Two Architectural Procedures' on pp 73–80 of the same volume.
9. Arakawa and Gins, *Reversible Destiny: We Have Decided Not to Die*, op cit, pp 77, 129.
10. Hector Oblak, 'The Unfindable Readymade', in tout-fait.com: The Marcel Duchamp Studies Online Journal, Vol 1, 1 May 2000.
11. Shaun Gallagher, *How the Body Shapes the Mind*, Clarendon Press (Oxford), 2005, pp 2, 5, 32.
12. Gins and Arakawa, *Architectural Body*, op cit, pp 75–6.
13. Shusaku Arakawa and Madeline Gins, 'Directions for Architectural Procedure Invention and Assembly', in *INTERFACES: Architecture Against Death/Architecture Contre la Mort*, double issue, Vol 1, Nos 21/22, 2003, pp 11–16.
14. Madeline Gins and Shusaku Arakawa (manuscript 2012), *Alive Forever, Not If, But When*. This book was begun and finished near to completion at the time of Arakawa's death. Madeline Gins is in the process of completing the text for publication.

Ginger Krieg Dosier, 1:1 biomanufactured brick, 2011
The brick was formed through a biomanufacturing process in which
bacteria induce calcium carbonate crystals that bind together and
solidify a mixture of sand, calcium chloride and urea.

Pia Ednie-Brown

bioMASON AND THE SPECULATIVE ENGAGEMENTS OF BIOTECHNICAL ARCHITECTURE

In the last decade, biotechnical architecture has become one of the most fertile areas for speculative architecture. Guest-Editor **Pia Ednie-Brown** traces the recent lineage of this field, highlighting the work of **Ginger Krieg Dosier and Michael Dosier of Vergelabs**, which has pushed biotechnical architecture further towards actualisation; their company bioMASON specialises in the biomanufacture of building material and its architectural applications.

85

It is hard to miss the power that the biological – or 'biotechnical imagination' – has in contemporary culture, and architecture has certainly not overlooked it. This has become particularly evident in the blurry bleed between digital and biological paradigms, with metaphorical associations, formal or processual mimicry, and other slippages between the two having a long history. Budding out of this historical relationship, we are now seeing the emergence of 'biotechnical architecture', where architects are exploring biotechnologies to engage directly with biological or living materials. Currently in a similarly nascent position to that of digital architecture in the early 1990s, this area of design exploration, as Oron Catts and Ionat Zurr point out in this issue (see pp 70–75), is still to be scrutinised. This lack of scrutiny is undoubtedly linked to the fact that there is very little on offer beyond entirely speculative or as-yet-unrealisable propositions. In some respects, this offers an opportunity to address the undeniably important role of speculative activity within architectural innovation.

However, one practice has pushed biotechnical architecture further towards actualisation than most, if any other, in the field. Ginger Krieg Dosier and Michael Dosier founded the experimental architecture practice VergeLabs[1] in 2006, and are now forming a company called bioMASON, specialising in the biomanufacture of building material and its architectural applications. In 2010, Krieg Dosier won the Metropolis Next Generation Design Prize to further her exploratory work into using bacteria, calcium chloride and urea to bind sand aggregate into bricks. In eradicating the high-carbon polluting heat-bake process of conventional brick production, this bacterial manufacturing method becomes significantly less environmentally problematic. The closer one looks, however, the more expansively this venture produces ripples in innovation ecologies. Combining grounded, actualisable proposals with wildly speculative propositions, this practice is notably innovative both within and beyond the discursive field of biotechnical architecture.

In order to more fully appreciate the significance of bioMASON, a brief and partial survey of how and where biotechnical architecture has, over the past five years or so, become a more visible presence in architectural discourse is required. This emerging trajectory gained some traction in 2008, with Marcos Cruz and Steve Pike's guest-edited *⌂ Neoplasmatic Design*. As Cruz and Pike noted in their introduction, there had been an accelerating cultural 'biologicalisation'[2] in the face of significant advances in biotechnology that architecture was yet to digest. They did not respond to this observation by claiming a coherent new movement and territory, or offering predictive visions. Rather, the publication simply aimed to collect 'a broad range of scattered design ideas and projects often dismissed as too speculative or simply project-hypothesis, and therefore currently unreported in architectural publications'.[3]

In 2011, Neil Spiller and Rachel Armstrong guest-edited *⌂ Protocell Architecture*.[4] They were now ready to stake out a territory, promoting 'protocell technology', which sits between artificial life and biology in the construction of chemical artificial cell systems, as the answer to 'a long awaited new beginning for architecture', as summed up in their introduction title: 'It's a Brand New Morning'.[5] Their introduction was followed by a manifesto based on Dadaist text, quite explicitly locating themselves in the avant-garde tradition.[6]

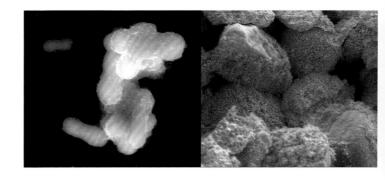

Sporosarcina Pasteurii bacteria, 10 microns, and cementation of sand
These rod-shaped (bacillus) *Sporosarcina Pasteurii* bacteria, which are naturally found in soil, are the living agents in the biocementing process of bioMASON's biomanufactured bricks. Attracted to the aggregate particles, they build a coating of calcium carbonate crystals around the grains. These same bacteria are also integral to Magnus Larsson's propositional project for the 6,000-kilometre (3,728-mile) long wall across Africa, with the idea that the bacteria would be injected into sand dunes to form sandstone structures. Along similar lines, Rachel Armstrong has claimed that protocells can be engineered to grow sandstone, a process that may be able to stop the sinking of Venice by coating the timber piles that underpin the city.

bioMASON logo, 2012
Ginger Krieg Dosier and her partner Michael Dosier, who together formed the experimental architecture practice VergeLabs in 2006, are now forming a company called bioMASON, through which they are scaling up the bacterial brick manufacture process towards mass production. Logo design by Nada Al Yafaei.

Having ideas seen to be worth spreading, architects Rachel Armstrong, Mitchell Joachim and Magnus Larsson have all done TEDTalks[7] about biotechnical architecture. All three presenters situated their proposals within rhetorics of environmental sustainability. Armstrong's talk (July 2009)[8] promoted protocells as the answer to crossing the divide between architecture and 'nature', stating that protocells, despite having no DNA, are living entities that can be chemically specified to respond in particular ways to stimuli, and thereby controlled towards particular ends. Joachim's TED talk (February 2010) was somewhat reminiscent of surrealist provocations, suggesting that we might engineer the growth of living tissue in producing new kinds of houses – from elaborately sculpted tree growth to meat houses where 'we use fatty cells as insulation, cilia for dealing with wind loads and sphincter muscles for doors and windows'.[9] He claimed to be the first architectural office of its kind, with a 'molecular cell biology lab' in Brooklyn. To be generous, Joachim's proclamations could be described as playful exaggeration, his far-fetched propositions being considered as part of a long tradition of utopian architectural fantasies inflected by formulaic TED styling.

Magnus Larsson's talk (July 2009)[10] presented his proposal for a 6,000-kilometre (3,728-mile) long wall across Africa, which as Geoff Manaugh has pointed out, puts it 'on a par with Superstudio's *Continuous Monument* – but with an environmental agenda'.[11] Working with the same kind of process as bioMASON, where sand particles are bound together with the use of bacteria, this wall has 'anti-desertification' environmental and political aspirations. Pictures of Larsson in the science lab were overlaid with the slogan 'to really appreciate architecture, you may even need to don a whitecoat' – a play on Bernard Tschumi (proclaimed by K Michael Hays as part of the 'late avant-garde')[12] and his 'Advertisements for Architecture' (1975), one of which pronounced: 'To really appreciate architecture, you may even need to commit a murder.'

As these examples indicate, the degree to which biotechnically inclined architects have worn the avant-garde mantle is notable. This is partly because architectural discourse is very used to utopian and avant-gardist declaration and will often recognise it as the face of innovation. The avant-garde tradition – part of the threadwork of Modernism – rests on a break with the past in aspiring for the new, and while we are certainly still feeling the avant-garde hangover, the 21st century has come to cast speculative activity into quite different conditions, where Modernist shocks and disjunctions are no longer able to do the same kind of work. Speculation has become an integral imperative of everyday capitalist culture, because so much hinges on debt, investment and capital gain, and because our tools for prediction, via complex simulations, have opened up the sense that we can act on all sorts of probabilistic knowledge about the future – with climate change being a prominent example. Speculation becomes a kind of datum for contemporary activity in that our decisions about what to do today are increasing and intrinsically based on what has not yet happened. In other words, the activity of generating speculative visions has itself altered in cultural status and impact – having been subsumed into the everyday.

As these examples indicate, the degree to which biotechnically inclined architects have worn the avant-garde mantle is notable. This is partly because architectural discourse is very used to utopian and avant-gardist declaration and will often recognise it as the face of innovation.

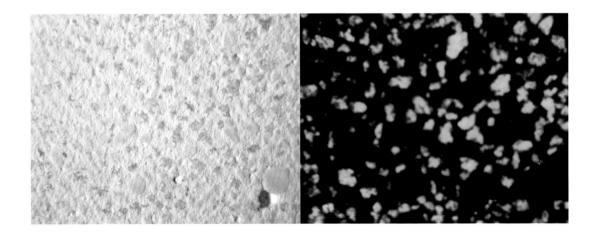

VergeLabs (Ginger Krieg Dosier and Michael Dosier), Glowcrete, 2007
This luminescent concrete, produced by VergeLabs, emits light by means of phosphorescent aggregate. This is one example of the experiments with architectural materials carried out by VergeLabs prior to the development of the biomanufacture process and bioMASON.

The kind of approach that Krieg Dosier and Dosier exemplify is linked, but not reducible to, the way in which VergeLabs – as the background to bioMASON – focused on experimentation *through* materials, such that ideas and speculations could unfold through tangible engagements. As Krieg Dosier conveys: 'We started off just basically … playing. We converted our second bedroom into a lab and just started playing with concrete, doing things like making glow-in-the-dark concrete, and weird balloon casting where we started spinning the form during the curing process. At the same time we were also taking classes in molecular gastronomy, working with chefs using liquid nitrogen and experimenting with how some food techniques might be used in producing formwork.'[13] From the start their emphasis was not on constructing a 'brand new' world or staking out idealised, uncharted territories, but to engage inventively and imaginatively with particularities – working not with the world as given, but as potential that might emerge through particular, situated conditions.

In 2009, Krieg Dosier participated in a SymbioticA Art and Science Workshop at RMIT University in Melbourne, run by Oron Catts and Gary Cass of the University of Western Australia. Krieg Dosier spoke about the importance of the open-source, DIY ethos that the workshop brought to the activities: 'The DIY culture allowed other researchers and myself a different mindset regarding standard laboratory tools, equipment and practices. As an example, expensive laboratory equipment – while at times essential – can also be made with off-the-shelf components. The immersion of this mindset was established the first day of the SymbioticA workshop, and was thematically carried throughout the week with open-source sharing among the participants.' This open-source, DIY, hacker or 'modding' ethos, where a range of familiar assemblages are hacked into, modified and refolded through one another, continues to be unfolded through the development of bioMASON.

We started off just basically … playing. We converted our second bedroom into a lab and just started playing with concrete, doing things like making glow-in-the-dark concrete, and weird balloon casting where we started spinning the form during the curing process.

SymbioticA Art and Science Workshop, RMIT University, Melbourne (conducted by Oron Catts and Gary Cass/University of Western Australia), November 2009
Ginger Krieg Dosier drills into a plastic container as part of a DIY workshop exercise to design and build a sterile hood. The sterile hood is standard equipment in microbiology and biomedical laboratories where materials need to be worked with in a sterile environment. An open-source, DIY, hacker or 'modding' ethos, encouraged in the SymbioticA workshop, becomes an important backdrop to the development of bioMASON.

Ginger Krieg Dosier, 2011
Having built a small laboratory at the American University of Sharjah in the UAE, Krieg Dosier was able to develop the biomanufacture process and explore its potential in depth. She has worked in numerous labs around the world in order to develop different aspects of the project.

The Metropolis prize in 2010 shifted Krieg Dosier's bacterial manufacturing experimentation out of the small, private laboratory spaces into a more expanded territory: 'The speculation is all great in the lab – it's really great that you're growing things – but once it turns into a reality and it's on the outside, you get a completely different set of people looking at it who are testing it to see, for instance, if it will actually outlast concrete or if it will crumble in the next rainfall.' Krieg Dosier was contacted by numerous companies and individuals from diverse backgrounds, including a farmer and a politician: 'My personal growth has never been so swift … I began forming a large team of advisors, scattered around the planet, to assist in directions for the various aspects of the work and business … After receiving the award, space and "real estate" required for the research grew exponentially, and I found myself landing in several satellite labs.' Moving between spaces and across voices, she was increasingly 'getting different fields and different voices in the room … it used to be just looking at how to get the sciences involved, but I'm learning that probably the most valuable player is the strategic planner. They're like an architect in the way that we like to combine trades and wear different hats – they do the same thing: they can play Devil's advocate, they can play your friend, your enemy, they can play psychologist … it's almost like a criminal investigation in some way.'

Conversations with various individuals who contacted her about the project led Krieg Dosier to explore the use of waste products, such as urea from the swine industry, mine tailings as a source of aggregate, waste egg shells from the poultry industry as a calcium source, and brewer waste yeast extract as a nutrient for the organism. This approach to the sourcing of materials acts to locate the brick product in what Krieg Dosier talks about as a kind of 'critical regionalism': 'the bio-brick material that I make here in the UAE is slightly different to the one that I would make in North Carolina because the different nutrients and waste resources slightly change the characteristics of the resulting material.' This also configures the production process as a complex, analogue parametric system – making it open to all manner of variation, such as a change in the chicken or swine feed altering the quality of the calcium or urea product entering the production system.

Once it turns into a reality and it's on the outside, you get a completely different set of people looking at it who are testing it to see, for instance, if it will actually outlast concrete or if it will crumble in the next rainfall.

Cemented glass beads
bioMASON brick production will initially focus on sand-based cementation, however the use of alternative additional aggregates that are determined to be waste products is also currently being explored. Recycled glass beads have emerged as one possible aggregate for future development. Due to their shape and composition, glass beads also serve as an analogue to sand for mineral isolation in scanning electron microscopy.

CT scan of biological cement tests of Mars simulant, NASA Ames Research Center, Moffett Field, California, 2011
This digital CT scan shows the distribution of aggregate (red) and cementing material (grey) in tests made using a Martian simulant. The Martian simulant is a blend of mineral aggregates from Hawaii that simulates the mineralogy, chemical composition, grain size, density, porosity and magnetic properties of what we know to be Martian soil.

The 'critical regionalist' aspect of the process takes on another life through the potential explored for bioMASON in space. In response to interest from NASA-ESA for a potential building material suited to the conditions on Mars, in 2011 they spent three weeks at the NASA Ames Research Center in Moffett Field, California, running some viability tests. Here they explored the idea of a double-shell inflatable formwork that could be filled with a bio-cementation media. The proposal they developed involved a swarm of robots that map soil conditions for appropriate aggregate while maintaining proximity to each other. Once the necessary resources have been located, the robots take root and inflate the formwork shell. Individual inflatables in proximity to one another deform their neighbours, creating differentiated clusters of rooms and forming cemented structures built with the local soil.

Scaling up towards mass production requires rethinking industrial spaces of manufacture, presenting quite unique requirements: 'It's an irrigation system that requires very simple raw materials and no energy supply – so one could imagine the units growing almost like hydroponics, with the important difference that hydroponics requires light and air circulation but the bio-bricks don't.' Krieg Dosier has visited a range of facilities to see how they get the highest yield in the minimum amount of space, speculating on the kind of facility that might be designed: 'Will a bio-brick factory look more like a very linear process where you have raw materials at the start and the bricks at the end? Or will it be a tower with bricks stacked? … Or maybe there's a cycle? … Scale-up is really the big question, but I'm not finding any a reason that it can't be manufactured in a large scale if you look at some precedents of hydroponics or farming, or hybrids of some of these different manufacturing practices.'

Another manufacturing process being explored comes from digital prototyping/3-D printing. Krieg Dosier discusses how she has 'always been interested in this material not being as homogeneous as a standard brick … you can control how much cement actually precipitates based on how much you feed it, so if you feed a certain area more – say, for example, the perimeter – you will get a harder material than the interior. In this way, you could print scaffolding or structural elements that are embedded in the material.' Krieg Dosier and Dosier are currently developing and testing a 3-D bio-printing device that can be programmed to feed specified areas of a given sand mass to generate differentiations in the cementation process.

In short, the development of bioMASON has involved generating multiple folds within and across a series of familiar spatial types, programmes and processes. Initially, by merging the architectural 'laboratory' with the scientific laboratory, they brought two quite different kinds of experimentation together. This was then opened up to a wider set of involvements, linking and folding together multiple spaces of production and knowledge: agriculture and farming, the corporate boardroom and strategic planning, industrial and space manufacturing, digital prototyping and biotechnology, and sustainability and waste recycling. Understated and restrained in one respect, and highly ambitious and speculative in another, bioMASON creates these folds in a manner that is situated and sensitive to local conditions.

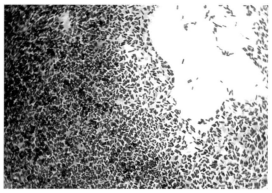

3-D bio-print device
top: Krieg Dosier and Dosier are developing and testing a 3-D bio-printing device that can be programmed to feed specified areas of a given sand mass to generate differentiations in the cementation process. *Sporosarcina Pasteurii* bacteria are mixed in a nutrient solution and placed onto the sand at programmed locations and depths.

Gram stain of *Sporosarcina Pasteurii*
right: The gram stain is a useful method for clearly viewing isolated bacteria and contamination with an optical microscope. Isolating one colony from a petri dish, a smear of bacterial cells is heat-fixed onto a glass slide. A primary stain of crystal violet is added and decolourised with acetone before a pink counter-stain of safranin is added to the slide.

This folding activity can be understood as integral to innovation ecologies and to that which makes bioMASON stand out in the field of biotechnical architecture. Theorist Robert Mitchell used the concept of 'the fold' to discuss cultural implications of the Bayh-Doyle Act, which was passed in the US in the 1980s with the aim of establishing a new 'innovation ecology'.[14] This controversial Act provoked major shifts through relatively simple means: by using patents as the medium of a 'stitch' that enabled and propelled business and research practices to enter into a codependent fabric of interactions. Mitchell suggests that folding offers a way of understanding both the way the Act operated, and the subsequent role of bioart within innovation ecologies. As he points out, even if bioartists will often operate as provocateurs or instigators of public awareness and debate, they are also inescapably implicated in the institutions and scientific practices that they provocatively critique. This can be regarded as a significant shift from the avant-garde model of innovation in that there is no 'break', no radical novelty and no separation, and as such:

the power of bioart emerges not as a function of its distance from, or its power to 'reflect on', the innovation ecology, but rather as a function of its ability to alter the flows of this ecology from within. Rather than critiquing this ecology from a separate and protected space, bioart instead appropriates the governing logic of this ecology, producing its own folds of information, money, and materials.[15]

By operating from within the ecology they seek to agitate, explore and bring to attention, bioart has some affinity with bioMASON's approach to biotechnical architecture, which proactively refolds the contours of existing cultural spaces, practices and architectural conditions – from within. However, unlike bioart, the aims are not related to any form of critique per se, being much more about creatively speculating in a material, affective process of unfolding potential. Through this approach, bioMASON manages to achieve what many other examples of biotechnical architecture do not: an engagement with the post-avant-garde, post-utopian nature of contemporary innovation ecologies, and in a manner that resonates with those very conditions.

Relative to other examples of biotechnical architecture, bioMASON is notable for the degree to which it manages to pursue the actualisation of speculative ideas. It would be a mistake, however, to understand this kind of work as being simply about application or reification. Rather, the difference they make boils down to a mode of speculative engagement that remains firmly in touch with both malleable actualities and the conditions that shape their potential. This situates their speculative propositions *inside* given conditions, creating transformations from within, in contrast with the implicitly externalised position of a more avant-gardist approach that aims to eradicate the mundanity of the familiar in order to forge the entirely new. bioMASON offers an alternative stance whereby the development of a specific technique can successfully link and create new interactions between distinct systems – setting loose multiple moving tendrils, each stitching, folding and generating conversations between otherwise relatively settled, separate areas of activity. ⚙

Notes
1. http://vergelabs.com/.
2. Marcos Cruz and Steve Pike (eds), ⚙ *Neoplasmatic Design*, November/December (no 6), 2008, p 8.
3. Ibid, p 14.
4. Neil Spiller and Rachel Armstrong (eds), ⚙ *Protocell Architecture*, March/April (no 2), 2011.
5. Ibid, pp 14–23.
6. Ibid, pp 24–5.
7. www.ted.com/talks.
8. Rachel Armstrong, 'Architecture that Repairs Itself?', TEDTalk, July 2009: www.ted.com/talks/rachel_armstrong_architecture_that_repairs_itself.html.
9. Mitchell Joachim, 'Don't Build Your Home, Grow it!', TEDTalk, February 2010: www.ted.com/talks/mitchell_joachim_don_t_build_your_home_grow_it.html.
10. Magnus Larsson, 'Turning Dunes into Architecture', TEDTalk, July 2009: www.ted.com/talks/magnus_larsson_turning_dunes_into_architecture.html.
11. http://bldgblog.blogspot.com.au/2009/04/sandstone.html.
12. K Michael Hays, *Architecture's Desire: Reading the Late Avant-Garde*, MIT Press (Cambridge, MA and London), 2010.
13. This and following quotes from the author's interview with Ginger Krieg Dosier, January 2012.
14. Robert Mitchell, *Bioart and the Vitality of Media*, University of Washington Press (Seattle, WA), 2010.
15. Ibid, p 61.

bioMASON manages to achieve what many other examples of biotechnical architecture do not: an engagement with the post-avant-garde, post-utopian nature of contemporary innovation ecologies, and in a manner that resonates with those very conditions.

Cities, and their component buildings and infrastructural systems, have developed rapidly in responsive and adaptive capacities. Ubiquitous computation and new informational technologies are increasingly embedded in the physical and social processes of the city. Here, **Michael Weinstock** identifies 'sentience', or the ability to be aware, as the primary driver of innovation in the urban environment; as the extended 'nervous system' of a city develops the potential to sense changes in the city's flows, and in its internal and external environments.

Cities are the largest and most complex artefacts constructed by humans. They are dynamic, spatial and material systems that display phenomena characteristic of complex systems – power scaling, self-similarity across a range of scales, and 'far-from-equilibrium' dynamics. All cities have an 'architecture' – an arrangement of material in space that changes over time as they are continuously repaired and rebuilt. They collapse and expand in uneven episodes of growth and decay, and their infrastructure and information systems are changed accordingly. From this perspective, cities are dynamic nodes on extended multiple networks through which energy, information and material flows.

There is a remarkable similarity between the mathematics of biological metabolism and that of urban metabolism, and in both the operation of metabolic systems occurs through surfaces and networks.[1] The pattern of energy flow through living forms, and through all the forms of cities, is subject to many fluctuations and perturbations. The flow is modified by 'feedbacks', but occasionally there is such an amplification or inhibition that the system must change, must reorganise or collapse. A new order emerges from the turbulence of the system that has collapsed. The reorganisation often creates a more complex structure, with a higher flow of energy and information through it, and is in turn more susceptible to fluctuations and subsequent collapse or change through reorganisation – a tendency of living systems and of cultural systems to ever increasing complexity.[2]

Phase changes occur in many kinds of complex systems, and it is widely agreed that new and innovative system properties emerge during transitions between well-connected and poorly connected phases in their networks. The effects of new informational processes and cultural practices in the 'network society' have resulted in changes to the way in which cities are inhabited, in particular popular practices that are characterised by temporary physical interventions, but also great information dissemination in mass social media, such as the Karneval der Kulturen (Carnival of Cultures) in Berlin. These changes are perhaps more significant than is generally acknowledged, and are changing the understanding of the city and its processes.

It was conventionally argued that individuals, or coherent teams of individuals, are the drivers of innovation, a common approach that structures the written histories of architecture and many other disciplines. This is epitomized by Frank Lloyd Wright or Le Corbusier, and has persisted into the 21st century with many practices such as Foster + Partners and Zaha Hadid Architects still taking the name of their creative leader. However, it is now widely argued that the cultural context and environment in which knowledge exists, the networks of connections through which information is transmitted and by which collaboration is effected, are very significant factors. Cities have been the primary location of innovations, and 'the dynamics of economic development and knowledge creation, among other social activities, are very general and appear as nontrivial quantitative regularities common to all cities'.[3]

The question arises: to what degree might cities and the global networks they inhabit be considered not just the location of innovation, but an active agent? Marshall McLuhan described global informational networks as something like an extension of the human nervous system, and suggested that the technology of transmitting information alters the perception and processing of its content. In his argument, early societies were characterised by the transmission of cultural information through auditory storytelling, where the transmission of knowledge is performed through social events. Printed materials then altered this situation, emphasising visual and linear thinking, individualism and fragmentation: 'print … fosters a mentality that gradually resists

any but a separative and compartmentalizing or specialist outlook'. In his view the emergence of the 'electronic media' would enable a new form of society with a collective identity – the global village interconnected by an electronic nervous system.[4] As such, the city becomes analogous to a living organism, as the anthropologist Claude Lévi-Strauss remarked in his memoir: *Tristes Tropiques*. 'It is at one and the same time an object of nature and a subject of culture; an individual and a group; something lived and something dreamed; the supreme human achievement.'[5]

From this perspective, the extended 'nervous system' of an individual city has the potential to enable it to sense changes in the city's flows, and in its internal and external environments, and to respond appropriately. The miniature embedded microprocessors originally developed as components of computers, cameras, cars and phones are now becoming ubiquitous in urban systems and environments, and in combination with advances in sensors, data management and transmission are a significant contribution to the evolution of sentient cities. Information systems are themselves rapidly evolving complex networks of connections between artificial nervous systems

The question arises: to what degree might cities and the global networks they inhabit be considered not just the location of innovation, but an active agent?

and the physical world. William J Mitchell argued that: 'We are also seeing the emergence, in the software world, of cognitive hierarchies similar to those exhibited in the operations of human minds.'[6] The integration of ubiquitous sensors and embedded intelligence, data flows and hierarchical software systems are critical to contemporary urban life, 'significant expressions of ideology, mediators of consciousness and instruments of power'.[7]

The evolving sentience of cities is beginning to bring about changes in the perception of public space and time, in engagement with performative and representational arts, and the dynamics of the city. The city is where we encounter other people, and it is the aggregation of formal and informal aggregations that animate the city and are intimately coupled to the patterns of life within it, and to the public spaces through which people flow. Cultural events and encounters are embedded in the intricate choreography of the evolution of cities, inflecting their evolutionary dynamics through processes of transmission

Kenzo Tange, Plan for Tokyo Bay, Tokyo, 1960
right: The design has an innovative approach to integration of its contributory systems through time, so that the spatial, programmatic and material dispositions are organised in relation to their relative durations and potential growth and decay.

far right: Detail model of the 'Civic Axis' indicating fixed elements of long-duration linear infrastructure of looping movement systems at different scales, permeated by shorter-duration and freer forms of buildings and urban surfaces.

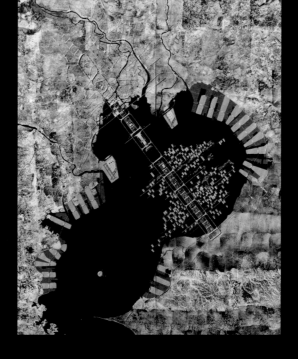

The architectural and urban manifestations of networks and new topologies, of fluidity and dynamics, are at the centre of architectural discourses and contemporary spatial innovations. The materiality of the boundaries between interior and exterior space, between public and private territories, is no longer so relentlessly solid and opaque.

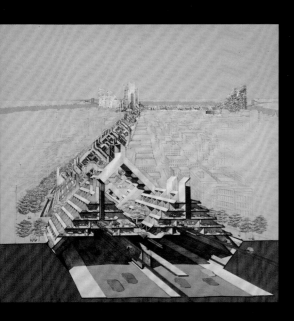

Paul Rudolph, Lower Manhattan Expressway, New York, c 1970
Movement systems and networks as the primary element of cities that included underground highways connected by moving walkways and escalators to shared public spaces and residences in one integrated and inhabited infrastructural system.

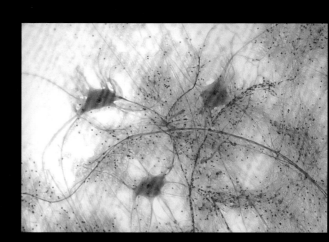

Synaptic pattern
Light micrograph of a cluster of neurons and connective dendrites from the grey matter of a human spinal cord. Surrounding the neurons is a mass of supporting cells collectively termed the neuroglia, which lends both mechanical and metabolic support to the nerve cells. The nervous system of the world has similar patterns.

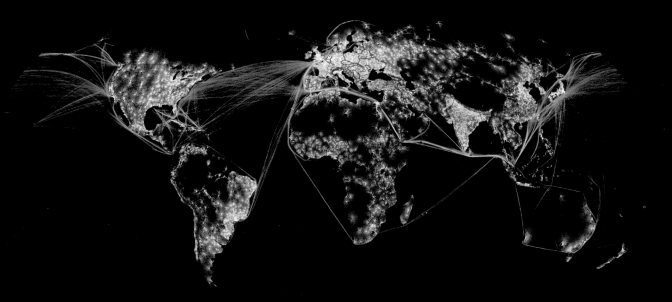

and dissemination, mutation and inheritance. The myths and images of the city, the utopian dreams and dystopian anxieties that synthesise societal dynamics with urban forms, are indexical cultural phenomena. The networks of public spaces through which people flow are the spaces of culture, the spaces in which culture is produced and on which culture reflects, and by which the social imagination of local communities and their spaces extend their engagement with information technologies and processes beyond their geographical boundaries.

The architectural and urban manifestations of networks and new topologies, of fluidity and dynamics, are at the centre of architectural discourses and contemporary spatial innovations. The materiality of the boundaries between interior and exterior space, between public and private territories, is no longer so relentlessly solid and opaque. The increasing transparency of such boundaries is accompanied by less rigid territorial demarcations. Programmes are not so strictly confined within the building envelope, and connections and coexistence are enhanced. The experience of being in spaces that flow one into another, with 'soft' transitions between private and public domains, and between interior and exterior space, is increasingly recognised as an essential characteristic of contemporary life. The largest public spaces, for example in the concourses of transit spaces such as airport terminals, ports and railway interchanges, have boundaries that are achieved less by rigid walls than by extended thresholds of graduated topographical and

phenomenological character, enhancing spatial connectivity and coded communication. This form of spatial organisation is increasingly found across a range of scales, from individual apartments through to new cultural spaces and urban configurations.

The vitality of cities is no longer dependent on the spatial and metabolic relationship with their local territory, but on the regional and global flows of resources and their connectivity to the global 'nervous system'. Extended conurbations are now common right across the world, consisting of several overlapping city territories that extend urban fabric across a range of scales, often coterminous with agriculture, industrial and energy generation territories. One of the best known conurbations in Europe is the Randstad, now more formally known as Deltametropool, connecting Amsterdam, Rotterdam, the Hague, Utrecht and multiple smaller towns into a continuous tissue that has a total population of over 7 million and covers an area of more than 8,000 square kilometres (3,088 square miles), with a very high connectivity of rail, road, light rail and tram networks. The overall configuration is a crescent-shaped linear chain that has a resemblance to the synaptic pattern found in living nerve tissues. The largest in the West is the Boston–Washington conurbation that has a population of more than 50 million. It, too, has a highly connected linear configuration of several large cities (Washington DC, Baltimore, Philadelphia, Boston and New York) and rather less dense overlapping subsidiary and suburban areas that constitute a continuous

As the networks evolve, new dynamics emerge within individual and linked cities, and the inherited hierarchies of spatial distribution, the relative sizes of urban elements and growth patterns have begun to change accordingly.

tissue. The very largest of all is in Japan, the Taiheiyo Belt, sometimes referred to as the Pacific Megalopolis, which ties together Tokyo, Nagoya, Osaka, Hiroshima and Fukuoka with a population of over 80 million people.

The flow of cultural information and energy has accelerated as the population of the world has expanded and the complexity of the world system continues to increase. The evolution and development of the urban systems of an individual city are accelerated or constrained by the flows between cities across the global network.[8] As the networks evolve, new dynamics emerge within individual and linked cities, and the inherited hierarchies of spatial distribution, the relative sizes of urban elements and growth patterns have begun to change accordingly.

There have been significant developments towards the development of sentience in individual buildings over the last decades, most notably in the capacity of automatic response to external changes in the environment, thermal self-regulation, and the integration and optimisation of building services and energy use. However, the number of buildings with responsive behaviour in any city is still very small when compared with the total built mass of the city, and cooperation between individual buildings to produce collaborative responsive behaviour at the scale of an urban patch or neighbourhood is rare. Moreover, it is clear that the path to sentient cities is not simply the aggregation of autonomous sentient buildings, but through their linkages to each other and to the infrastructural systems of transportation, water, energy, communications, waste collection and disposal, 'green' and public spaces. The development of sentience in the separate infrastructural systems of the city, and their integration into a 'metasystem' to which sentient neighbourhoods are coupled, has yet to be achieved, although it is hypothesised that the critical threshold of phase change in cultural systems and informational technologies is current and is driving the collapse and reorganisation of inherited systems from which sentient cities will emerge.[9] △

Notes
1. Michael Weinstock, 'The Metabolism of Cities: the Mathematics of Networks and Urban Surfaces', George Legendre (ed), △ *Mathematics of Space*, July/August (no 4), 2011.
2. Michael Batty, 'The Size, Scale and Shape of Cities', *Science* 5864, 2008, pp 769–71; Michael Weinstock, 'Metabolism and Morphology', in Michael Hensel and Achim Menges (eds), △ *Versatility and Vicissitude*, March/April (no 2), 2008, pp 26–33; and Michael Weinstock, *The Architecture of Emergence: The Evolution of Form in Nature and Civilisation*, John Wiley & Sons (Chichester), 2010, pp 130–7.
3. Luís MA Bettancourt, José Lobo, Dirk Helbing, Christian Kuhnert and Geoffrey B West, 'Growth, Innovation, Scaling, and the Pace of Life in Cities', *Proceedings of the National Academy of Sciences*, Vol 104, No 17, 2007, pp 7301–06.
4. Marshall McLuhan, *The Gutenberg Galaxy: The Making of Typographic Man*, University of Toronto Press (Toronto), 1962.
5. Claude Lévi-Strauss, *Tristes Tropiques*, Librairie Plon (Paris), 1955, trans John Weightman and Doreen Weightman, Jonathan Cape (London), 1973, p 155.
6. William J Mitchell, 'Intelligent Cities', *UOC Papers*, Issue 5, October 2007: www.uoc.edu/uocpapers/5/dt/eng/mitchell.pdf.
7. Ibid.
8. Celine Rozenblat and Denise Pumain, 'Firm Linkages, Innovation and the Evolution of Urban Systems', in Peter Taylor, Ben Derudder, Pieter Saey and Frank Witlox (eds), *Cities in Globalization: Practices, Policies and Theories*, Routledge (London), 2007, pp 130–56.
9. Michael Weinstock, 'Sentient Systems and the City', in △ *System City*, forthcoming, 2013.

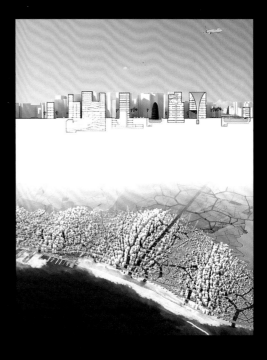

Jens Pedersen and Andy VanMater, Hydrological City for Qatar, Emergent Technologies and Design Thesis, Architectural Association (AA), London, 2011
above and opposite: Evolutionary model for variable density city in Qatar, driven by growth of the canal network as the primary infrastructural system that integrates evaporative cooling for the microclimate, floating stills for freshwater production, and all other city distribution and collection subsidiary systems.

FINAL DRAFT

DESIGNING ARCHITECTURE'S ENDGAME

'Completion is both essential for, and antithetical to, innovation.' Here, **Gretchen Wilkins and Guest-Editor Andrew Burrow** attempt to resolve this generative paradox by going in search of 'open-to-ending strategies in architectural practice'. They advocate the model of the 'final draft' in the design process as a means to bringing a project to a close while anticipating or encouraging future work.

Isn't keeping things unfinished the most open and the best way of getting things done? Certainly, it is a generative design path that was advocated in the 1990s by the likes of Greg Lynn, Brian Massumi and Michael Sorkin when the introduction of digital software advanced the possibilities of a new level of experimentation and iteration. See, for example, Massumi's analysis in this issue (pp 50–55). Of course, this all depends on what is meant by 'done', and the reasons to stay undone are changing.

A telling starting point for what is meant by done is the term 'final draft'. Firstly, because the two words bring into tension the completion and incompletion of the same entity. Secondly, because it hints at an indirection. Namely, the possibility to resolve this tension by imagining a sequence of 'drafts' that stand apart from the 'final' object, so that finality is reduced to a stopping of the drafting process. It is a very useful term for this reason, even if conflicted, and an incredibly vital space for design to operate within, even if elusive; we know design may begin anywhere, but can it also end anywhere? If final drafts indicate that a piece of work is effectively done, but not finally, they also indicate future potential within that work (more than the termination of it). They say, 'this is done, but there is more to be done' and hand the work over to the next. If endings are then designed with this agenda, to anticipate or encourage future work, then incompletion and completion might coexist as two sides of the same coin, strategically as well as incidentally. This article is a search for some of the open-to-ending strategies in architectural practice.

The dilemma is this: completion is both essential for, and antithetical to, innovation. Production is a prerequisite for innovation – new ideas, things or methods emerge from existing complete ones. Yet, innovation is by definition concerned with transformation and change – nothing can be taken as complete, and everything remains open to become source material for further development. In this sense, to innovate is to see things as incomplete. This essay seeks to show how, in architecture, the most amenable approach is to create conditions that allow for the intensity and focus of individual authorship while introducing the annealing benefits of creative and collective input, for work to be done, but not necessarily end.

Then, what are the ways we can reach the final yet stay in draft? It is helpful to think about three realms in which these tactics can manifest. Firstly, there are tactics in the material realm, those present in the final object by virtue of its deployment of materials. Secondly, there are tactics in the representational realm, those present in the draft itself either by virtue of the need to put it into play in order to realise the material design, or by virtue of a fluency in the language of the drafts themselves. Finally, there are tactics that relate directly to either, but only after transformation by innovation. Once we are clear on what these might mean, we will be close to the very core of this issue.

It is relatively simple to locate a few of the key tactics in the material realm. We can create things that contain material that is unallocated, subject to reallocation, or even raw in some sense; for example, the partially constructed meals of a Swedeish smorgasbord or Chinese hot pot, or the generic rooms of a single-fronted cottage. These commonplace tactics of incompleteness are useful in themselves, but also point by analogy to tactics in the other two realms.

It is less simple to locate the definitive tactics in the representational realm. One can justifiably forgo an attempt at enumeration of tactics: any sufficiently expressive representational scheme will contain the seed of self-reference which, like a hall of mirrors, quickly generates a cascade of reflections. Instead, think first of the straightforward opportunities that arise in the move from representation to material realisation. In this case, we can choose representational schemes that are: abstract or generalised, and thus subject to specific instantiation; open or indeterminate, and thus subject to interpretation; or generative, and thus non-deterministic in their outcome. Architecture is a fertile ground for such tactics because there is a great role for representation and its interpretation. The disparity in cost between drafting a design and realising it as a building elevates the role of representation in architecture to the point where it sustains its own discourse. For example, consider the absurd paradoxical spaces of Giovanni Battista Piranesi (1720–78) or the joyful speculations of Archigram. So, we can think next of the opportunities that arise within the representational realm, and work by analogy from tactics for incompleteness in the material realm, thus treating the draft as material in its own right. We can open the next question by considering what forces are at work to put rawness in the representation to work.

Elemental, Quinta Monroy, Iquique, Chile, 2001
above and opposite: The Elemental housing projects of Alejandro Aravena exemplify the power of incompletion in the material realm. The project responds to funding shortfalls in public housing by constructing exactly that half of a house that scaffolds the remainder.

Buildings awaiting an urban fabric, Detroit, Michigan, 2006
The stoic exterior of the Grand Army of the Republic (GAR) building in Detroit yields nothing to the severe urban fluctuations that have taken place around it. Now standing as a fragment of the former urban fabric, the interiors have been appropriated for many cultural uses since its construction in 1900.

Awakening to the tension in the term 'final draft' offers a way towards these ends, by encouraging a deliberate focus on production without the crisis, or conceit, of finality. In summary of the above, the territory of finishing becomes a focus, either by letting go earlier or by embedding mechanisms to prompt future work, both of which focus on strategising the endgame of design and production. Alejandro Aravena's response to financial shortfall in social housing in Chile is a striking example: 'When you have money for half a house, the question is which half do we do?'[1] This is distinct from crowd- or open-sourced processes, although it learns much from those principles. In the case of open-source software, the imperatives are to extend the reach, change the performance, and perpetuate the project, even by cloning (forking) where necessary. Hence the appeal: fork me! In place of a tension between final and draft, the tension is between contribution and cloning. Looking at it another way, adding designers is a strategy that balances dilution of voice against stimulation of incompleteness, whereas cloning a project is a strategy that balances dilution of effort against vigour of the pool of competing projects. In the strategy of final drafts, the aim is to maintain control over a (relatively) complete piece of work while instigating a next phase, and not to situate design within a fully open or perpetually adjustable system. Final drafts mediate this inherently conflicted boundary; they are not nascent, mutable or tentative, nor are they fixed, permanent or absolute. They are creatively incomplete.

Godsell & Corrigan, Refugee Family Unit, 2011
Godsell & Corrigan is the nom de plume of unknown provocateurs. These images operate entirely within the representational realm of architectural practice in Melbourne, wielding representation to satirise both style and content.

Final drafts help us navigate this inherently conflicted boundary by introducing a pair of countervailing forces. In short, they reflect the forcefulness required to assert our work to others. The key is to comprehend two aspects of a group design process. The first aspect concerns the establishment of meaning. The group immediately imbues a level of ambiguity to every novel design act in the sense of Donald Davidson's accounts of meanings: it sends the others scrambling to adjust their translations of our new design moves.[2] The second aspect concerns agency. Navigating the territory of finishing requires illocutionary force in the sense of John R Searle: acting to assert finality is an attempt to change the state of the draft by pronouncement.[3] The two are not entirely compatible, and hence can be seen as countervailing forces. In this way, they afford finer control over the trajectory of a design process.

Why is now a good time to reappraise the value of incompletion? For one thing, as the economic, ecological and social challenges grow, so does the complexity of design objectives. In particular, sustainability, of any type, demands greater interdependence between once-separate elements. In turn, this necessitates more specialised designers acting in more complex networks. Simultaneously, there has been a cultural shift towards participatory tools relating to the rise of the web (see Mario Carpo's observations on p 56–61 of this issue). Together, these forces suggest more networked designers. It is argued above that designers must tune their skills in the territory of finishing to gain finer control over the trajectory in such settings. The final draft as a technique contains an image of the designer as both a 'black box' and a 'white box' element in the network. When asserting finality, the designer is incorrigible concerning the status of the draft, and thus a black box;[4] when openly drafting, the designer is a white box open to inspection. The key to acting in the new networks and navigating their shifting connections is performing this switching to best effect, namely to adroitly manoeuvre in the territory of finishing. These concerns play a further role in navigating the shifting contractual arrangements that determine how buildings are delivered. As the roles of developers, builders, financiers and clients shift in these structures, designers will find themselves operating in new positions in larger networks of stakeholders, and the same arguments for working in the territory of finishing can be expected to hold.

Cities in the world that have been great cities in my lifetime have gone through legendary phases in which they offer cheap ground-level retail space and cheap live-work space for young artists. They no longer have it in the same way. They've become sort of cooked. And once a city is completely cooked, it's more like Paris, where the city's business is not to change. But it's not a place that actually welcomes innovation.
— William Gibson, 2012[5]

Unfinished cities engender innovation. Depending, once again, on what is meant by 'done', the types of cities that most readily fit this description are not always new or not-yet-finished cities; it is not a function of being undeveloped, but being open to change. Even mature or stable cities can grow to become unfinished as a result of severe economic, industrial or environmental shifts. Detroit is an example, over 300 years old and still uncooked by many definitions including Gibson's, with no lack of cheap ground-level retail space and (consequently) much opportunity for innovative design practice. As such, inverting the original statement may offer the best definition of the term: cities that engender innovation are unfinished, and assert their 'draft' state as 'final' in order to perpetuate continued innovation.

In this case, being unfinished is posed as an agenda rather than a description. Cities should strive to remain unfinished – in central districts, and not just the urban peripheries. The momentum of growth in any major city would suggest this is impossible, but is it? Cannot the best qualities of unfinished cities be (re)inserted into the mature, less affordable ones? How might architecture and urbanism embody incompleteness, even if their city is already cooked?

Even mature or stable cities can grow to become unfinished as a result of severe economic, industrial or environmental shifts.

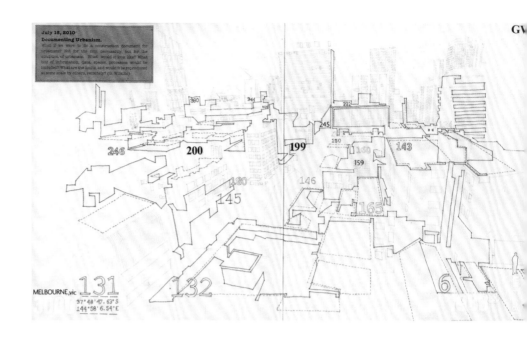

As a pilot project, the Passport Project tests agency
within the strategy of final drafts in an adaptable format,
combining tangible evidence with open-endedness, and
individual with collective authorship.

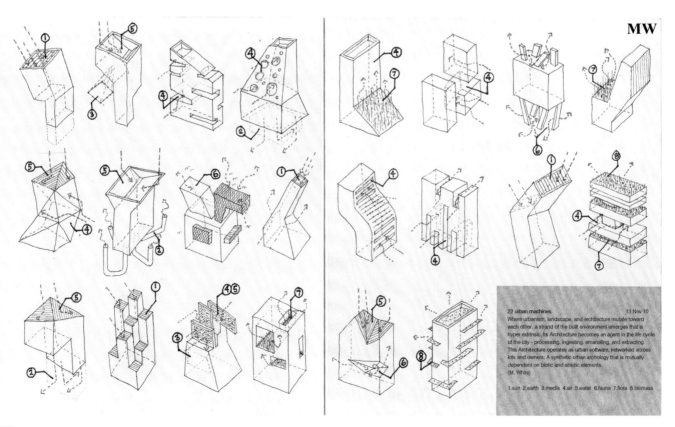

The paradox may be resolved through the mechanisms of planning, if unofficially so, by strategies that resist full economic, architectural or infrastructural cohesion. Embedding interpretative measures or 'incompleteness' into regulatory codes, for example, keeps the policies guiding urban development in 'draft' state until 'completed' or evidenced through building, of which multiple translations are possible. This may involve reprioritising the balance between qualitative and quantitative criteria in building and planning policies. For example, Michael Sorkin's account 20 years ago is well worth revisiting.[6] Material execution is a forceful assertion of finality, of being done, while simultaneously awaiting change through appropriation. Practices of prototyping, incentivising property and plot ratios or temporary constructions also work towards greater diversity in use and value of urban space. William Lim outlines a strategy for incentivising plot ratios in Singapore and rapidly densifying Asian cities in his book *Incomplete Urbanism*.[7] These approaches are most attractive when they are most necessary, during economic recession, but the longer-term effects are where the real value lies. This is because they do not seek the normative, linear process, but enact building as a way towards regulatory change rather than the other way around. Dan Hill's Low2No project with the Helsinki Design Lab/ SITRA is a recent example of prototyping to instigate policy change.[8] The building demonstrates, rather than describes, the effects of alternative approaches, a reversal of the typical project process. However small or ostensibly provisional, these projects act as Trojan horses for greater, longer-term change.

World's Fairs are another example. Expo buildings are constructed quite literally as final drafts – full-scale prototypes in public use, but without the risks of long-term commitment. However, they often remain in use, sometimes indefinitely. In this sense, they are a provocative reversal of the strategy of final drafts, asserting the status of draft even when final. The Royal Exhibition Building in Melbourne, for example, was built for the 1880 International Exhibition and continues to host events today. Another famous example is the US Capitol building, designed and constructed separately by 10 different architects over 77 years, with another six architects contributing since its declared completion in 1868. But perhaps the peerless champion of incompletion is Antoni Gaudí's Sagrada Família in Barcelona, which, in the decades-long search for completion, has afforded an outstanding laboratory for experimentation in digital design and construction techniques.[9] The final building will be the material embodiment of sustained cycles of feedback between past representational intent and future material possibility. Construction-as-research projects such as these produce robust architectural, technological, representational and material experimentation. Yet, they are not deliberately designed to be incomplete, and this is precisely the point. Striving towards completion is critical, and yet incompletion proves vital to what comes next. The final draft as a strategy of practice enables this.

The Passport Project

As a pilot project for testing modes of collaborative authorship and engagement within the subject of urbanism, the Passport Project was launched in 2010. Curated by Gretchen Wilkins in Melbourne to include an international network of contributors, its aim is to produce a global project comprising discrete, individual contributions documenting local urban conditions. It takes the form of a book that travelled to 24 people in 23 cities and 18 countries over 676 days, collecting construction documents for urbanism. This method intentionally combines qualitative material with qualitative outcomes, frustrating the relationship between design, representation and (future) production. Each contribution identifies and documents a trigger for particular urban conditions without telling the whole story; each is a fragment of a larger conversation about urbanism produced through data, machines, anticipation, alchemy, anamorphosis, identity, war, resistance, childhood, collisions, memory and flux.[10] As a pilot project, it tests agency within the strategy of final drafts in an adaptable format, combining tangible evidence with open-endedness, and individual with collective authorship.

Gretchen Wilkins, 'Construction Document for Urbanism', Passport Project, Melbourne, 2010

opposite top: What if we were to do a construction document for urbanism? Not for the city, necessarily, but for the condition of urbanism, whatever that suggests. What would it look like? What bits of information, data, spaces, processes would be included? How would we determine the 'city limits', and how might the document act as a template or set of instructions to be reproduced at some scale by others, remotely?

Mason White, '22 urban machines', Passport Project, Toronto, 2011

opposite bottom: Where urbanism, landscape and architecture mutate towards each other, a strand of the built environment emerges that is hyper-extrinsic. Its architecture becomes an agent in the lifecycle of the city – processing, ingesting, emanating and extracting. This architecture operates as urban software, networked across lots and owners; a synthetic urban archaeology that is mutually dependent on biotic and abiotic elements.

Composite sample of the Passport Project entries, 2011
Each entry is a study of triggers of urban change. From top left to bottom right: Charles Anderson (Melbourne), Jonathan Solomon (Hong Kong), Thomas Daniell (Kyoto), Moira Henry (New York), Pablo Garcia (Pittsburgh), Katie Morris (Baltimore), Louise Ganz (Belo Horizonte), Adrian Duran and Mario Baez (Montevideo), Gerardo Caballero (Rosario), Sarah Calburn (Johannesburg), Mireille Roddier (Paris), Lluis Sabadel Artiga (Girona), Riet Eeckhout (London), Kristine Synnes (Haugesund), Sandy Attia and Mateo Scagnol (Bressanone), Amit Talwar (New Delhi) and Chris Knapp (Byron Bay)

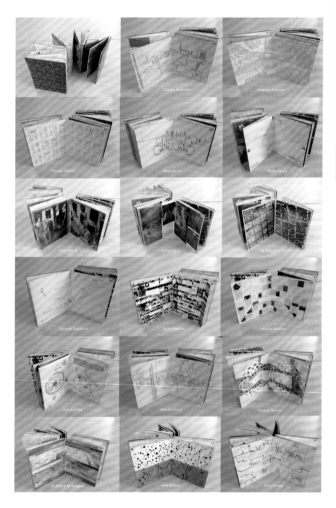

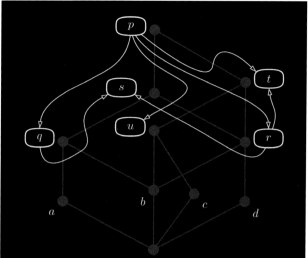

Unlike many other disciplines, collective authorship and deliberate strategies for creative incompletion in architecture are not immediately obvious, applicable or widely taught.

Perry Kulper, Alchemic Urbanism, Passport Project, Ann Arbor, Michigan, 2011
A series of key words best describes this image: over-coded; erased; gold; leafed; residuals. Soft; orange; metro; blooms; waiting. Shadowed; evasive; speeds. Milled; surplus; data. Documenting; bleached; out; blue; networks. Trapped; marble; glances. Extracting; compressed; cyclical; rhythms. Tracing; fabricated; acrid; velocities.

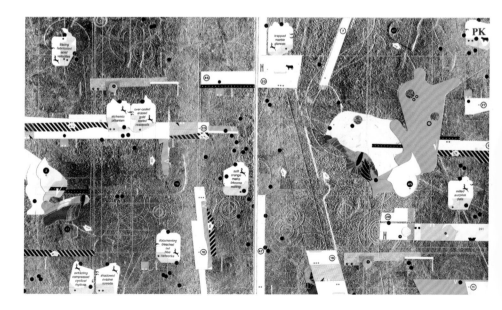

Snakes and Ladders in the Network of Collaboration

The above has argued the role of the final draft in navigating the inherently conflicted boundary between control and conversation as designers increasingly find themselves working in networks. However, the article cannot conclude without addressing the role of how we represent networks and, in particular, how this affects the development of network expertise.

There is a danger in the uncritical use of computing metaphors to depict collaboration in design. We should be clear which ideas are privileged when depicting how networks of designers resolve ideas and develop authorship. The strategy of final drafts depends on saying 'done!' It is dependent on conversation; it entails a cascade of switches between draft and final that assemble subordinate decisions and consult varying subsets of the team. A designer's performance emerges across those settings in which he or she participates, not just from saying 'done', but also from advocating for the incomplete. Then, the image of a network carrying discrete messages like parcels of information is unhelpful. Instead, a more helpful diagram depicts the groups through which a designer passes as he or she creates and communicates. There is already some work on this approach,[11] and the strategy of final drafts promises a fresh evaluation of this alternative diagram.

Finale (Not Final)

Unlike many other disciplines, collective authorship and deliberate strategies for creative incompletion in architecture are not immediately obvious, applicable or widely taught. The strict regulatory, legal and financial conditions through which the profession and industry operate all but disallow it. This does not mean there is no place to rethink these principles, however, or that methods of doing so are already prescribed elsewhere (in computation, for example). Architecture comprises a vast collection of practices, each of which has an ending point, and each ending is an opportunity to strategise the next.

Collective authorship need not replace the inevitable, and invaluable, masterpiece or signature work. Instead, we advocate a parallel practice specifically structured to engender completeness and incompleteness at once, to participate individually in a collective practice. Signature work asserts finality in the face of ongoing drafts; it is a forceful statement of being done despite the fact that new appropriations, uses, interpretations and alterations will inevitably prove that a signature final is, in fact, an 'exquisite' draft. Collective systems of design are so conducive to innovative practice because they provoke unintended consequences by nature. They embody the innovation imperative. Indeed, to design a framework for collaborative production is to design a machine for more innovative practices. ⚲

Andrew Burrow, Snapshot of a hypertext structured over a lattice of participants, 2004
opposite top right: In this diagram, four participants represented by the letters a to d are working on a hypertext comprising pages represented by the letters p to u. Each grey circle stands for the set of participants collected by following grey edges downwards to a label. The diagram explicitly identifies how the text is split between subgroups, and which hyperlinks cross between subgroups.

Notes
1. Alejandro Aravena, quoted in Justin McGuirk, 'Alejandro Aravena', *Icon*, Vol 67, 2009, p 56.
2. Donald Davidson, 'Radical Interpretation', *Dialectica*, Vol 27, 1973, pp 314–28.
3. John R Searle, *Expression and Meaning: Studies in the Theory of Speech Acts*, Cambridge University Press (Cambridge), 1979, pp 1–29.
4. Richard Rorty, 'Incorrigibility as the Mark of the Mental', *Journal of Philosophy*, Vol 67, 1970, pp 399–424.
5. William Gibson, quoted in Alex Pasternak, 'William Gibson in Real Life', *Motherboard-TV*, 4 April 2012; http://motherboard. vice.com/2012/4/4/motherboard-tv-william-gibson-in-real-life
6. Michael Sorkin, *Local Code: The Constitution of a City at 42° N Latitude*, Princeton Architectural Press (New York), 1993.
7. William SW Lim, *Incomplete Urbanism: A Critical Urban Strategy for Emerging Economies*, World Scientific (Singapore), 2012, p 62.
8. Dan Hill, Low2No project by SITRA and the Helsinki Design Lab: www.low2no.org/.
9. Temple Sagrada Família: http://sagradafamilia.sial.rmit.edu. au/.
10. Passport Projects: http://passport-projects.com/.
11. Andrew L Burrow, 'Negotiating Access Within Wiki: A System to Construct and Maintain a Taxonomy of Access Rules', in *HYPERTEXT '04: Proceedings of the Fifteenth ACM Conference on Hypertext and Hypermedia*, ACM (New York), 2004, pp 77– 86.

Leon van Schaik, Ideogram, April 2012
To the left is a profile of a protagonist in the field of vital
architecture. Behind the head is an arc of internalised
presumptions. To the right is a series of fans depicting
a series of choices: political or ideological, mode of
engagement, form of service, front-of-mind outcome and
manner of designing. Projects fall out below and work
their way back to reconfigure the presumptions.

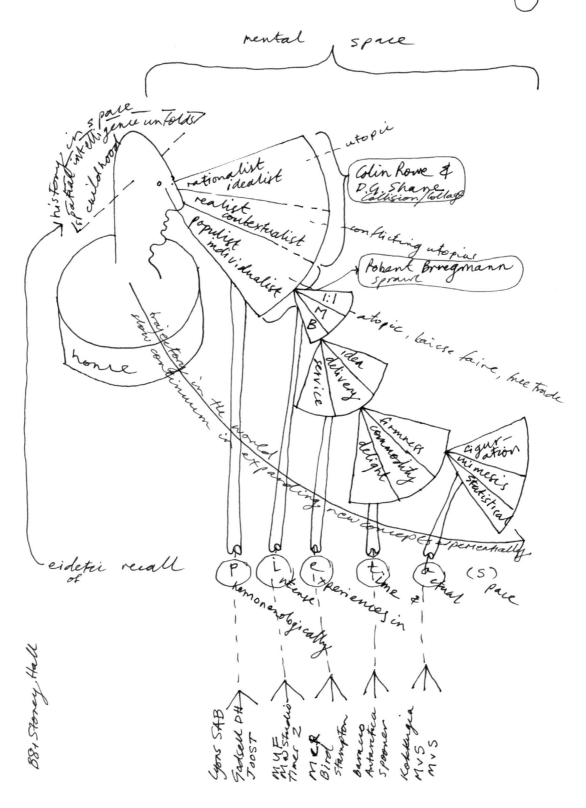

DIFFERENTIATION IN VITAL PRACTICE

AN ANALYSIS USING RMIT UNIVERSITY OF TECHNOLOGY AND DESIGN INTERFACES WITH ARCHITECTS

One of the most influential figures in architectural education and practice today, **Leon van Schaik,** Professor of Architecture (Chair of Innovation) at RMIT in Melbourne, has dedicated the last two decades of his career to the promotion of local and international architectural culture through design practice research and the commissioning of building. Here he describes how he has nurtured a research-oriented approach through his engagement with a network of 'vital' practitioners worldwide who are interested in strong ideas and pushing the questioning of the status quo.

For 25 years, working from RMIT in Melbourne, I have engaged with innovative architectural practices, developing an understanding of how their differentiation is supported by being in a community of practice in which three substantively different – tripolar – approaches to architecture are being pursued.[1] This research into design practice is conducted through RMIT's design practice research PhD programme, a programme that invites practitioners with a peer-recognised body of work to engage in reflections on the nature of the mastery that they have established, its trajectories and the social structures that sustain it; and then to speculate on possible futures for practice arising from a deeper understanding of its processes. The research also flows through my own initiatives and research into ways of commissioning innovative architecture. My experience indicates that innovative communities of practice tend to thrive when at least three alternative and differentiated positions are actively operating as part of the constitution of that culture. As such, I have undertaken to analyse the community with which I have been engaged in terms of a tripartite model of differentiation, and to promote these differentiations within that community in helping to foster its ongoing vitality.[2]

My encounters with architects have been in four spheres: commissioning architects, researching the design practices of architects, moderating the studio offerings of architects within the school of architecture, and in writing critical appreciations of works of architecture for monographs and for the professional media. A consolidated list brings the total number of practices across those spheres to just below 200. Included in this list is a small but significant group of architects from Singapore and Malaysia. Also present, but not included in the numbers, are about 30 architects currently engaged in design practice research, many of whom are based in London and in other parts of Europe. In the commissioned/commissioning sphere, there are 45 practices, and in the design practice research there are 90 architects.[3] The studio-leading and critiqued spheres have involved a further 45 practices each. Clearly, this community of practice is not geographically bound, but all have something in common – that is, a research-oriented approach to their practice. These practices tend to be interested in questioning the status quo, pushing limits, being experimenters – or 'vital' practices. Such practices are described as 'strong idea' practices as distinct from 'strong delivery' or 'strong service' practices.[4]

This consolidated group can then be split into three groups: those whose design outcomes demonstrate an *idealist* political stance, those whose works suggest a *realist* position, and those whose works are *populist* in intent. This is an inexact process, as architects may adopt different stances in different circumstances. As will later be demonstrated with specific examples, for every project an architect will adopt an 'implied author/implied audience' position; in some instances this varies widely from project to project (probably a realist situation as we shall see), and in others not at all (probably an idealist stance).

What is meant by these political categories? Where architectural works suggest a perfectible universe achievable through the extended designing of the architect, there an idealist approach is detectable. Such authors have in mind a perfected world, and in their projects they realise fragments of that perfected world. It is as if their design ideas shine down dimly over the entire surface of the world and glow into life when a project is realised. This is a Whig position, first argued for in England as Palladianism emerged as a world-architecture. The belief here is that the universe can be understood, and that we should act on that understanding, doing all in the light of reason or, rather, 'rationality'. 'Reason' suggests an empirical scientific position, such as that espoused by popularising physicists. But there are distinct limits to the utility of reason brought to bear on understanding the universe through architecture. Even as they promote different ways of being in the world, architectural propositions tend to represent the understandings of physicists rather than create new views of the nature of the universe. Intense concern with the 'turning the corner' is symptomatic of the idealist architecture position, and Mies van der Rohe's masking of contingent structural reality with symmetrical arrays comes to mind. While reality is masked, the appearance of rationality is achieved.

Whig theorists despised what seem to us virtuoso Neoclassical buildings such as Christopher Wren's Trinity College Cambridge Library (1676–84). In this two-storey structure, a lofty reading room on a heavily arcaded base collides pragmatically with the much squatter three-storey sides of the quad it forms. Such pragmatists are realists who shine the light of their reason into a dark and murky world, and seek to fix only what they can. They eschew the totalising rationality of idealists and quite happily fake a dome – as at St Paul's Cathedral in London (completed 1711) – in order to achieve a desired outcome or effect. The world is a mess, will always be a mess, and we are at our best muddling through. This is the Tory position. Edmond and Corrigan's book *Cities of Hope* (1993) crystallises some specific thinking behind a realist architecture, showing how the architect launches arks of redemption onto the turbulent oceans of an imperfectable world.[5]

Minifie van Schaik (MvS), Cloudnets I and Cloudnets II, 2008–
opposite: Practitioners at MvS work in two contrasting modes. Paul Minifie uses statistical thinking as his driver, and delivers projects from this angle. His research into city development uses Cloudnets to model possible futures.

The populists are strangely ignored in many analyses, as in the idealist/realist duality deployed above. Populists were there, forming a crucial third pole in the actual, if not in the parliamentary, politics of the day, and were bloodily suppressed. The later Chartists (1838–48) are in this pole, and there is some evidence that Australian attitudes to urbanity were formed by the transportation of Chartists to the colony. Some have traced the lingering attachment to standalone fabric in the Australian imaginary to the Chartist belief that the only protection from the rapacious state ordinary individuals could have was to own their own property. In England in the 1960s, the work that architect Walter Segal (1907–85) did to enable people to self-build well-designed homes stands out, as does the self-build movement in favelas and townships around the world. In my analysis, populist architects are those who work from such individual desires rather than from state, institutional or corporate objectives. Often they have an art-practice background, one that gives them the autonomy they seek in order to work in this way; muf is an example in the UK. The sample analysed divides into the following segments: idealist (30 per cent), realist (60 per cent) and populist (10 per cent).

Look now at the full sample (around 200 practices) through two different takes on the ways in which they design. The first take asks whether they designed in a *full-scale 1:1* way, prototyping, setting up site design offices (as Ralph Erskine did for the Byker Wall in the mid-1970s), tracing sites in real time as an anthropologist might (mass observation like). The second take seeks out those whose mental space and designing is primarily based on *virtual* mediums. These can be used intuitively (simply accessing digital platforms) or with *statistical thinking* (finding underlying rule systems, designing algorithms that replicate them and seeking formally un-premeditated outcomes).[6] The third take clusters together those who use the normative skill set of architectural practices today in a *bricoleur* way, most using traditional means, others challenging these by admixing tools from other mediums, such as filmmaking.

My experience indicates that innovative communities of practice tend to thrive when at least three alternative and differentiated positions are actively operating as part of the constitution of that culture.

muf Aus, DIY Park, Mornington
Peninsular, Melbourne, 2008
top: The DIY Park on the Mornington
Peninsula south of Melbourne is an exemplar
of a full-scale prototyping project harnessing
in populist fashion the design energies of
the community it serves.

McBride Charles Ryan, Cloud House,
North Fitzroy, Melbourne, 2011
middle: Representation of a 'strong idea'
project.

Here muf Aus is an exemplar of full-scale working, setting up site offices in the midst of the communities they design for, using community insights to identify design opportunities, and using full-scale urban furniture to effect local dreams of civility. So are Richard and Michelle Black in their site-based works. Minifie van Schaik (MvS) encompasses two positions with Minifie bringing abstract statistical thinking to bear, notably in his research into urban development, and van Schaik using collages of approaches in his designing, bringing projects to fruition, and relating them to their physical and social contexts. This time the sample divides full scale 10 per cent, virtual 10 per cent, and bricolage 80 per cent.

Behind these tripolar positions lies the ancient architectural triad postulated by Vitruvius: 'Firmness, Commodity and Delight'. *Firmness* relates to the principle of parsimony: simplest possible plan and structure, least use of materials. *Commodity* is primarily concerned with serving and expressing social need. *Delight* suggests a fascination with the theatrical enhancement of being in the world. Here the full sample divides firmness 20 per cent, commodity 53 per cent, and delight 27 per cent.

The next analysis, with reference to another duality identified by Li Shiqiao,[7] but adding a third term, looks at how the architectural outcomes could be classified according to three modes of designing: *figuration*, *mimesis* and (a third term imported from the previous analysis) *statistical thinking* of the mathematical rather than the naive kind. These could be seen to relate to the ancient categories, and this needs teasing out. Figuration appropriates figures that exist and recomposes them as collages of varying degrees of directness. Mimesis identifies admired precedents, seeks out the processes that have given rise to them, and seeks to replicate those processes with results that seldom mimic the originals. And statistical or abstract thinking seeks out new understandings of hidden orders and uses those to generate designs, often devising automata to drive the formal invention. Here we see figuration of many degrees of appropriation and recombination in the work of Peter Corrigan, McBride Charles Ryan and muf Aus; mimesis in the work of Richard Stampton and Baracco Wright; mimesis and statistical thinking in the work of M@Studio and MvS; statistical thinking underpinning the Greening Australia and exurban studio teaching of Baracco and in the designing of Baracco Wright; and statistical thinking succumbing to figuration in the work of kokkugia. Here, the 'strong idea' was used again, and the sample divides figuration 57 per cent, mimesis 29 per cent, and statistical thinking 14 per cent.

Edmond & Corrigan, Building 8, Melbourne, 1994, and ARM,
Storey Hall, Melbourne, 1994
RMIT's pioneering criterion-based selection process commenced with
the procuring of Building 8 and Storey Hall. These and other RMIT
buildings have become markers in the mental space of architects in
Melbourne.

Of course each pole differentiates within itself: the collages in figuration could be 'stock'[8] or cliché; naive or spontaneous and unselfconscious;[9] or as knowing and conscious as in artist Richard Hamilton's system of ensuring that each component in a collage was pared back to the threshold of recognisability before being put into a mix. Mimesis is similarly analysable, and statistical thinking bifurcates into a triad at the very moment that its systems deliver architectural form. These analyses provide clues as to how architectural practices differentiate themselves within a vital architectural culture. The differentiations are all examples of what RMIT Senior Research Fellow Dr Marcelo Stamm describes as 'constellating' creativity.[10] Mindful of Bruno Latour's argument that facts are created by projections of understandings, and then by discovery,[11] this investigation concludes by speculating on the differentiation between several Melbourne practices, some fairly well established, some very new.

Tabulating the analyses shows that to grasp differentiation properly, we need to make an informed speculation about the 'mental space' of each architect: that mix of learned canonical influences and the history of the unfolding in actual places of each architect's spatial *intelligence*.[12] This interaction is the focus of research currently underway in collaboration with RMIT Professor SueAnne Ware. The analyses above help define the canons that each practice holds dear, because each mode has its histories writ in the products of architectural culture, built and unbuilt. And the specifics of these canons are very revealing: differentiation becomes evident in the first 'top of mind' mentors, international and local, that practitioners mention. For example, three of these practices mention Lacaton and Vassal as internationals, but their local exemplars are different. The ways in which an architect's spatial intelligence capability unfolds is complex. We can, however, show how most 'fast thinking'[13] of a spatial kind is unconscious (we call it intuitive) and situated behind the mind's eye (see the ideogram here) until brought into play by research such as that conducted by architect Allan Powell, who documented the haunting of his imagination by many unheroic spatial situations in a seaside suburb of Melbourne where he has spent his childhood and his adult working life; of Robert Simeoni who has documented the informal architectural inventions of his community of north Italian migrants as they converted 19th-century architecture into a simulacrum of Italian Modernism; and in Belgium architect Jo Van den Berghe, who, once persuaded of the significance of his spatial intelligence, worked back from one characteristic design strategy – a penchant for designing circulation systems with a scissor stair athwart the direction of travel – to a precedent in his early childhood. During a practice research symposium in Ghent in 2010, I recall that he exclaimed after discovering this deeply embedded precedent: 'You don't know what you know, till you find out!'

Joost, Queensberry Square, Melbourne, 2012
The temporary pavilion at the Melbourne Food Festival is an exemplar of a populist/individualist project.

Antarctica, Community House, Flowerdale, Victoria, 2012
below: Built after the major fires in Victoria, the Community House illustrates the firm's concern with community 'commodity'.

StudioBird, AlphaOmega Apartment, Melbourne, 2008
centre: The interior demonstrates architect Matt Bird's fascination with the use of humble materials in decorative arrays – innovative delivery is the keynote here.

Michael Spooner, Swimming Pool Library, Melbourne, 2011
The proposal concentrates its energy on theatrical and literary 'delight' in a manner that resonates with the work of CJ Lim in London.

I conclude with a tentative analysis of a few vital practices currently at work in Melbourne. Their innovation is evidenced in their work, examples of which are illustrated. How they position themselves within the local community of vital practice, and therefore in the communities of such practice elsewhere, is the purpose of this analysis. The argument is that innovative vitality is forced by the process of differentiating from peers, mentors and challengers, both local and international. The analysis clusters practices that are differentiated by politics, mode of practice and manner of designing. Where these coincide, the differentiation shifts to the architects' virtual communities of practice (the international-admired and the local-admired).

Combined, these mappings chart the mental space of each architect and reveal differentiation at work even where most factors are held in common. Thus Michael Spooner and Matt Bird share political stance, mode of practice and manner of engagement with Roland Snooks of kokkugia, and are thus in the same bracket. The different spins they put on each of these qualifiers is revealed by the differing internal mentor identified by the local affinity they nominate. Spooner and Bird are in an early emergent position. However, kokkugia, in the same bracket, are more established and are in a community of practice with M@Studio and MvS (Minifie) whose manner and internal mentors are markedly different, but whose local affinities are linked. MvS (J van Schaik) is then associated with a community of practice including McBride Charles Ryan, muf Aus and Joost by a shared interest in popular architecture, with outcomes differentiated by politics, mode and manner, by internal mentoring, by local affinity or lack thereof. Baracco, Antarctica, Stampton, Simeoni and Times Two share politics, mode and manner and are differentiated chiefly through local affinity, partly through international mentoring. This group inhabit a community of practice defined on the one hand by the emergence in Melbourne of RMIT's commissioned architecture,[14] and on the other by the link between muf Aus and muf UK. ⌀

Notes
1. Leon van Schaik, *Mastering Architecture: Becoming a Creative Innovator in Practice*, Wiley Academy (Chichester), 2005, pp 106–9.
2. Leon van Schaik and Geoffrey London with Beth George, *Procuring Innovative Architecture*, Routledge (London), 2010, p 30.
3. Other disciplines at RMIT – Landscape, Fashion, Interior and Industrial Design – account for the published total of over 100 practices studied.
4. John Heintz and Guillermo Aranda-Mena, 'Business Strategies for Architectural Firms: Type Versus Capabilities', International Conference of Management of Construction: Research to Practice, Montreal, 26–29 June 2012.
5. Conrad Hamann, *Cities of Hope: Australian Architecture & Design by Edmond and Corrigan*, Oxford University Press (Oxford/Auckland/New York), 1993. See also the new and more comprehensive edition edited by Fleur Watson that includes a major essay by Leon van Schaik: Leon van Schaik, 'The Ambition to Make the Culture', in Fleur Watson (ed), *Cities of Hope Remembered Rehearsed*, Thames & Hudson (Port Melbourne, Australia), 2012, pp 166–9.
6. Daniel Kahneman, *Thinking, Fast and Slow*, Allen Lane (London), 2011.
7. Li Shiqiao, 'Memory Without Location', *Fabrications: Journal of the Society of Architectural Historians, Australia and New Zealand*, Vol 19, No 2, April 2010; and Li Shiqiao, 'Mimesis and Figuration Large Screens, Cultural Creativity and the Global City', in William SW Lim (ed), *A Collection of Essays on Asian Design Culture*, AA Asia (Singapore), 2009, pp 18–24.
8. Ivor Armstrong Richards, *Practical Criticism: A Study of Literary Judgment*, Harcourt Brace & World (New York), 1956.
9. Orhan Pamuk, *The Naive and the Sentimental Novelist*, Faber and Faber (London), 2011.
10. Leon van Schaik (ed), *Architecture & Design, By Practice, By Invitation: Design Practice Research at RMIT*, second edition, onepointsixone (Melbourne), 2012.
11. Bruno Latour, cited in Barbara Hernstein Smith, 'Dolls, Demons and DNA', *London Review of Books*, Vol 34, No 5, 8 March 2012, pp 25–6.
12. Leon van Schaik, *Spatial Intelligence: New Futures for Architecture*, John Wiley & Sons (Chichester), 2008.
13. Daniel Kahneman, op cit.
14. Leon van Schaik and Geoffrey London with Beth George, op cit, pp 14–28.

Innovative vitality is forced by the process of differentiating from peers, mentors and challengers, both local and international. The analysis clusters practices that are differentiated by politics, mode of practice and manner of designing.

Tom Daniell

THE MO
OF INV

THEPO
ENTITON

Japan-based architect and academic **Tom Daniell** puts out a call to architects, beseeching them not to lose sight of their role as creative inventors. Rather than being diverted into despair by the present confluence of ecological, economic and political crises, architects should be providing much needed optimism, thinking beyond the current situation with utopian visions. He challenges the view that future innovation is to be located in collective collaborations, regarding 'true innovators' to be individuals, such as Rem Koolhaas, Hernan Diaz Alonso or Philippe Rahm, who provide the essential entrepreneurial catalyst for the interaction of other people and ideas.

If necessity drives innovation, then there has never been a more challenging time to be an architect or a greater need for innovative architectural thought. The world is supposedly at a moment of crisis, or a confluence of crises, a perfect storm of ecological, economic and cultural conflicts. We face urgent challenges caused by rapid globalisation and urbanisation, demographic and technological transformations, material and energy scarcities, natural and all-too-human disasters. This is a time for the profession to display seriousness and sobriety, yet it is precisely at such a time that 'speculative' – a word intended to evoke both conjecture and risk – architectural proposals are most valuable.

Conversely, prosperity and peace are not necessarily detrimental to innovation. During Japan's economic bubble of the late 1980s, for example, spectacular architectural experiments were enabled by fantastically wealthy and progressive clients, jumpstarting the early career of idiosyncratic talents like Shin Takamatsu, who was encouraged to indulge his most arcane compositional whims. Intelligent, restrained creativity was compelled by the ensuing crash, delaying the early career of practices such as Atelier Bow-Wow, whose lack of work forced them to develop a research methodology that provided the conceptual foundation for the ensuing buildings.

Each cycle of bust and boom never returns us to where we started. At best, the temporarily imposed austerities become ongoing habits – the price of petrol may come back down without us ever returning to the former level of consumption – and our design repertoire is permanently widened by the invention of ad hoc techniques and concepts.

There is a well-known urban legend about calculations made in the 19th century that prove some major city (usually London or New York) will soon be covered with a deep layer of horse manure, a consequence of accelerating migration from the countryside and the spread of horse-and-buggy technology among the less privileged. Echoed today by anxiety about increasing car ownership in China, it is a nice parable on the vanity of attempting to predict the future by extrapolating current trends. Nevertheless, while architects necessarily respond to demographic, technological and attitudinal shifts that have already taken place, they are expected to make anticipatory design proposals for a better future.

The accumulating data about resource depletion and environmental degradation deserve our full and constant attention, but conservative action should be bolstered by radical thought. Despite all the sober talk about new mandates and responsibilities – the sour-grapes epitaphs for spectacular forms, the demotion of the individual genius and promotion of synergistic collaborations, the noble or opportunistic manifestos for being cheap and green, and the admirable pro bono work for those genuinely in need – the incontestable urgency of ecological issues is no excuse for despondency, anxiety, or timid designs. The architect is always fundamentally an optimist, and architectural design is always fundamentally utopian. While the percentage of the built environment directly produced by architects is insignificant, the indirect influence can be huge. Each successful experiment inspires widespread imitation and sets standards for others to follow, eventually making the original invention unremarkable, if not banal. One only need think of the way that the once-shocking innovations of Le Corbusier and Mies van der Rohe soon became part of the repertoire of every architect.

In the engineering community, innovation is generally defined as a novelty that has commercial potential, but the field of architectural design has been more often than not advanced by eccentric individuals pursuing their own interests without regard for rationality, sustainability, economy or personal financial gain (recall the financial turmoil and intermittent poverty or bankruptcy in the lives of figures such as Antoni Gaudí, Frank Lloyd Wright, Charles Rennie Mackintosh, Louis Kahn, Thom Mayne and Will Alsop). While the motivations for innovation may be broadly divided into the exigencies or opportunities arising in the wider world and the personal obsessions or compulsions among designers, there is also a school of thought that, somewhat counter-intuitively, sees innovation as potentially arising through a reduction in authorial control. Design is here the act of initiating then guiding more or less autonomous processes, such as using computer-based genetic algorithms in the development of architectural forms, accommodating the inherent, unpredictable tendencies of physical materials, permitting builders to improvise their own solutions on site, and facilitating the collective intelligence and decision making of a distributed group.[1]

No one denies that the larger or more complex the building, the greater the team effort its realisation entails. Like the auteur film director, the 'starchitect' (surely the laziest shibboleth of politically correct architectural criticism) stands at the peak of a pyramid of supporting players whose anonymity and replaceability increases as the pyramid widens. Overt creativity and charisma aside, true innovators often act as entrepreneurial catalysts for the interaction of other people and ideas. They bring into being shifting webs of collaboration, the effects of which continue to resonate well beyond any one project. Disproportionate credit being given to the individual genius tends to be a result of thoughtless journalism and the public's fascination with celebrity, rather than dishonest claims of sole authorship. Even the relentlessly innovative Rem Koolhaas has always tried to downplay the cult of personality, giving his office a mock-corporate acronym, working in fluid partnerships, meticulously listing collaborators and team members each time a project is published, and taking every opportunity to acknowledge their importance. Documenting the design process of the 1989 Très Grande Bibliothèque project for Paris, he writes: 'Beyond all exploitation, there is also altruism at work: OMA – machine to fabricate fantasy – is structured for *others* to have the eurekas.'[2]

Just as no one ever creates something truly alone, what is created is never truly unprecedented, always entirely contingent on more or less direct historical lineages. Innovation is a product of constant deviation and hybridisation, enabled by wider cultural and technological change. Contemporary visualisation and fabrication techniques have opened almost limitless sculptural possibilities for architecture, locking much of the profession into an increasingly frantic pursuit of the remaining reserves of new form, grasping at ever-finer distinctions or ever-more extreme distortions. The results are often transient novelty rather than fundamentally new, a sophisticated styling of shapes without the risk of real change.

However indirectly, the potential for genuine innovation in architecture is ultimately manifest in work that intensifies and elaborates the conventional realm of architecture (form, space, structure, material, detail) or else in work that expands the boundaries of that realm into territories that are conventionally considered to be non-architectural. The former category ranges from the kind of formal flamboyance (in the everyday as well as the art-historical sense) exemplified by Hernan Diaz Alonso's Xefirotarch, to the extreme distillation of structural and material performance found in the objects and buildings of Junya Ishigami. The latter category includes the exploration of invisible, insubstantial effects in the 'meteorological' architecture of Philippe Rahm, as well as the deliberate incorporation of unexpected, usually undesirable elements such as the moss and dirt in the buildings of Terunobu Fujimori.

With a position in the current architectural discourse analogous to that of Piranesi's 18th-century *Carceri d'Invenzione* etchings – unbuilt but hugely influential, arguably reflecting the underlying mental condition of the era – the architecture of Xefirotarch is grotesque yet mesmerising, like lifting a rock only to find noxious, swarming insects from which one cannot look away. Descending from Peter Eisenman's insistence on the autonomy of form via Greg Lynn's emphasis on virtuoso technique, the repellent, pornographic quality of these images prevents them from ever becoming a comfortable backdrop, constantly challenging the nervous system and aesthetic sensibility of viewers. Ignoring or deferring any realistic concern with structure, material or function, the usual order of precedence is reversed: function follows form, or at least they enter into a strange improvisational dance, an architectural *folie à deux*. The impact is in how it looks, but the innovation is in what it does.

Xefirotarch, TBA 21 Museum Pavilion, Patagonia, Argentina, 2011
Designed for the barren landscape at the foot of the Andes, the museum is intended to trigger a mutation of programme via the mutation of form, described by the architect as 'horrific-becoming-beautiful'.

Junya Ishigami, KAIT Workshop,
Kanagawa, Japan, 2008
This single-storey glass-clad student hall on
a university campus contains a seemingly
random array of 305 white-painted, thin
steel bars, some in compression and others
in tension, in order to precisely balance
the roof.

Also reliant on parametric computation, but for entirely different aims, the work of Junya Ishigami, a former apprentice of SANAA, comprises elements that seem suspended or merely touching, lacking any plausible means of support. This is structural exhibitionism by omission – not the manifest agility of a gymnast, but the illusions of a stage magician. From his debut 2004 Table (a thin sheet of steel made to span 9 metres (30 feet) by giving it a camber that settles flat under its own weight), to his Balloon installation (a one-tonne armature of aluminium framing and skin made weightless with precisely the right amount of helium), to the KAIT building (an almost-flat roof sitting on a forest of thin steel bars, their orientation and thickness cumulatively strong enough to support it, but only just), Ishigami's work is a didactic demonstration of the limits of material performance. The more extraordinary the effect, the less noticeable it is – his house proposals seem to leave the surfaces of their sites untouched, like fragile open-topped boxes turned upside down and placed lightly on the ground, giving no hint of the sophisticated foundation systems that this entails. The potential for innovation here arises from conventional methods presented with such reductive clarity that they again become revelatory.

The potential for innovation here arises from conventional methods presented with such reductive clarity that they again become revelatory.

Drawing on the ecological insights of Reyner Banham and the pneumatic architectural experiments of the 1960s, Philippe Rahm produces nuanced physiological effects that act on the skin rather than the eyes, categorising his work with terms more common in mechanical engineering than architectural design: radiation, conduction, convection, pressure, evaporation, digestion. Passive and active climate-control techniques conventionally used to produce homogeneous interior environments are instead deployed to create experiential variety in illumination, temperature and humidity. Architectural design has always been about the creation of appropriate moods, but Rahm operates directly on the atmosphere (understood in material, not metaphorical, terms), indirectly forcing innovation in the composition and performance of the building envelope.

Philippe Rahm, Convective Condominium, Hamburg, Germany, 2010
Using hot air's natural propensity to rise, the apartment is designed with terraced floor slabs and different ceiling heights to create a thermal landscape with variations in temperature available to its occupants.

Rahm produces nuanced physiological effects that act on the skin rather than the eyes, categorising his work with terms more common in mechanical engineering than architectural design.

Philippe Rahm, Evaporated Rooms, Lyons, France, 2012
Apartment refurbishment designed on the basis of naturally occurring atmospheric gradations in section, with furniture and functions situated at differing heights for appropriate temperatures and light intensities.

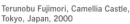

R&Sie(n), Dustyrelief/B_mu (facade construction detail), Bangkok, Thailand, 2002
left (both images): A project for an art museum in Bangkok, for which the architecture was to be wrapped in an electrically charged wire mesh that would attract and collect airborne pollution, gradually forming a thick, shaggy layer over the entire building.

Terunobu Fujimori, Camellia Castle, Tokyo, Japan, 2000
below: A public tasting room for a *shōchū* (clear distilled spirits) producer, the building is covered with plant life, with grass in the diagonal joints of the stone cladding and a camellia tree at the apex of the roof.

Terunobu Fujimori, Flying Mud Boat, Chino, Japan, 2010
bottom: Built adjacent to a museum holding a retrospective exhibition of Fujimori's work, and since relocated to his own property, this tea house is clad in copper and mud, and hoisted on cables like a hammock – a realisation of his long-held dream to build architecture that floats in the air.

However primitive or naive it appears, Terunobu Fujimori's work is radical in the literal sense, a return to the roots of architecture and a rethinking of construction from first principles. While his buildings tend towards an archaic simplicity of form and vernacular construction techniques, they are distinguished by the deliberate, controlled infestation of plant life. Weathering here is not merely a romantic aestheticisation of the accumulation of patina, but a manifestation of cyclical renewal as the building envelope sprouts and sheds over the course of each year. More extreme examples may be found in the work of R&Sie(n) and [eIf/bʌt/c] (both practices led by François Roche), such as Dustyrelief/B_mu, a project for an art museum in Bangkok that would use electrostatic forces to collect particles of atmospheric pollution into a shaggy, growing layer on its exterior, or the Thing Which Necroses pavilion, made of bioplastic panels that rot away. The necessity for green thinking here transcends technological, rational solutions towards a vivid expression of ecological interconnectedness and perpetual innovation.

These four distinct modes of practice – the libidinous, unapologetic id of Diaz Alonso, the sterile, precisely controlled superego of Ishigami, the civilised hygiene of Rahm, the raw atavism of Fujimori – are not, of course, without peer or precedent. Each is a prominent example of wider design research projects being undertaken throughout the profession. Clearly divergent in their aims, they are not always mutually exclusive. While conceptual hybrids are often infertile or stillborn, there are architects able to vividly combine aspects of all these approaches, as in Toyo Ito's Taichung Metropolitan Opera House (and its earlier incarnation as the Ghent Forum): simultaneously a convoluted, porous form evoking a slice of coral or foam and an optimised structural shell of minimum thickness, the building is to be covered with greenery and conditionally open to the outer world, using passive environmental techniques to modulate the interior climate and flows of matter and energy across the exterior membranes. Radically innovative at every level, it is projects such as this one that instigate transformative shifts in the evolution of the entire discipline.

Not all the work described here is so successful, yet it presents a range of confident deviations from the norm – small steps and giant leaps – wherein innovation does not refer merely to new technological products, but to provocative, dynamic pathways open for others to explore. To many people, these practices may seem trivial, hermetic or irrelevant, but they are best understood as analogous to, say, Formula 1 racing: on the one hand, it is a pointless and wasteful indulgence for a tiny audience, but on the other hand, it is the source of most of the innovations that are constantly transforming the field and benefiting us all, thanks to the enthusiasm of a small group of fanatics within the automobile industry (as with avant-garde architecture and the construction industry). If the task of the speculative architect is to strike out alone and explore uncharted territory, the question of which particular directions will lead to the most useful outcomes is not only unanswerable, but probably counterproductive. Best to delay as long as possible before seeking accountability from architecture's innovators, or judgements from architecture's critics. ⚏

Notes
1. Such approaches are being well documented in ⚏. See, for example, *Design Through Making* (July/August 2005), *Programming Cultures* (July/August 2006), *Collective Intelligence in Design* (September/October 2006), *Neoplasmatic Design* (November/December 2008), and the present volume.
2. Rem Koolhaas, 'Strategy of the Void', in OMA, Rem Koolhaas and Bruce Mau, *S,M,L,XL*, 010 Publishers (Rotterdam), 1995, p 644.

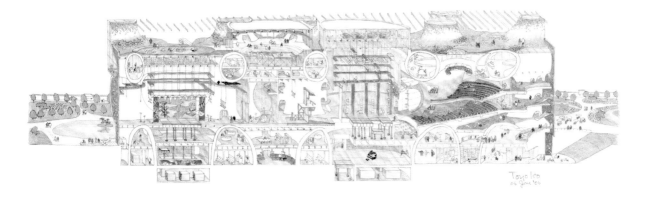

Radically innovative at every level, it is projects such as this one that instigate transformative shifts in the evolution of the entire discipline.

Toyo Ito, Taichung Metropolitan Opera House, Taichung, Taiwan, due for completion in 2013
Currently being built by the Taichung City Government and composed of three-dimensionally curved concrete shells, the architecture is a virtuoso experiment in spatial and formal continuity, open to its surroundings in all directions, allowing the movement of people, matter and energy across its internal and external membranes.

Terry Cutler

DESIGNING TOMORROW'S INNOVATION

Chair to the Australian government's Review of the National Innovation System in 2008, **Terry Cutler** is an industry consultant and strategy advisor with a background in the information and communications technology sector. Here, he opens up the question of architectural innovation to the wider context of the economy and social need. If architects are to innovatively address pressing social and environmental issues, such as climate change, obesity, population ageing and resource depletion, how does the architect's role need to be reformulated?

Poster for *Soylent Green*, 1973
Soylent Green, starring Charlton Heston, is an entirely dystopian view of future society in an overheating world short of food and water. The film is a *cri de coeur* calling out for more positive design innovation as an antidote to the effects of over-population and overconsumption as depicted in the film.

Most of us readily agree that innovation is a good thing, but we tend to be less critical and discriminating about the hows and whys of innovating. This issue of △ is timely because architects and designers should be asserting a stronger, less defensive stance about their role in meeting contemporary innovation challenges.

There is a paradox with innovation. On the one hand the logic of market capitalism tells us that innovation, the turf wars over productivity and competitiveness, is mandatory for the survival of market capitalism as we know it. This is true: Joseph Schumpeter's dictum about innovation as 'creative destruction' keeps shaping the ever-changing marketplace.[1] On the other hand, the successful, incumbent beneficiaries of market forces – those who came up with yesterday's good idea – relentlessly resist assaults on their current market dominance and monopolies, like bloodthirsty lionesses protecting their patch and their brood. Early on in the evolution of modern market

systems, Adam Smith, he of fame for his book *The Wealth of Nations*,[2] cannily identified the irresistible allure of cartels and monopolies for successful entrepreneurs.

Today, this dialectical struggle between protectionism and adaptive change has intensified, as the debate changes from being only about the economic form of market structures and institutions to one about societal sustainability – the very survivability of the wider frameworks underpinning capital markets.

Thus discussion on the topic of innovation has shifted from an investigation of the operation of markets to a debate about the sustainability of our social structures in the face of the unforgiving 'wicked problems' that now beset us. These wicked problems include the seemingly intractable challenges of urban congestion, pollution, environmental degradation and climate change, obesity and chronic disease and unwellness, population ageing, and resource depletion – both of energy and food. Traditional market economics and innovation practice have not evolved to address this level of complexity, not least because these problems are global problems, not redressable by localised or individual action alone. No one agent, operating alone, can advance a solution, an efficacious innovation.

This contemporary dilemma exposes structural weaknesses in our societal frameworks for knowledge management, problem solving and innovation. In addressing the crises of cities and of congestion, mobility and sociability we need to re-create the vibrancy and vitalities that drove the social imperatives to urbanisation in the first place.

Posing the contemporary innovation challenge in these terms puts architecture and design right back in the spotlight. In responding to this challenge architects and designers need to tackle three issues: How to shape solution scenarios that super-ordinate the specialisation of knowledge and skills; How to accommodate professional practices within broader collaborations; and How to find and nurture the 'natural organisers' of holistic solutions and compelling teleological scenarios of possible futures.

Adam Smith's identification of the specialisation of labour as the drive shaft for modern capitalism has proved indisputable. He was also prescient in anticipating its adverse consequences and the need for counterbalances. Everywhere we operate within bureaucratic silos and build fences around our specialised expertise: we know more and more about less. Intellectually and operationally we are like caged animals in an institutional zoo.

Architecture and design has not escaped this balkanisation. Design specialisations have developed around fashion, industrial design, graphic design, interiors and landscapes, and architectural functions have become dispersed across surveying, engineering and project management.

To offset the downsides of the specialisation of endeavour, Adam Smith identified the need for a class of people who would specialise in 'knowing everything':

those who are called philosophers or men of speculation, whose trade it is, not to do any thing, but to observe every thing; and who, upon that account, are often capable of combining together the powers of the most distant and dissimilar objects.[3]

Here, Smith succinctly summarises many of the functions of the innovator: that person with that breadth of attention so as to be able to 'connect the dots' and produce combinatorial novelty – the very substance of innovation.

In the spin jargon of management consultants and university business schools we now advocate the production of 'T-shaped' people who combine breadth and depth. Discard the spin and this is a profound and important challenge. How do we reinstate the polymath or people who can rise above disciplinary or professional blinkers? Two exemplary role models stand out.

The first exemplar is Vitruvius, who observed that the architect must combine theory and practice. The architect's service 'consists in craftsmanship and technology'. Vitruvius's description of the well-educated architect is both inspiring and a savage critique of today's narrow specialisations. He articulated the model of the 'undisciplined' architect thus:

Let him be educated, skilful with the pencil, instructed in geometry, know much history, have followed the philosophers with attention, understand music, have some knowledge of medicine, know the opinions of the jurists, and be acquainted with astronomy and the theory of the heavens.[4]

Many centuries later, John Maynard Keynes described the attributes of a master economist in remarkably similar terms:

The master-economist must possess a rare combination of gifts … He must be mathematician, historian, philosopher – in some degree. He must understand symbols and speak in words. He must contemplate the particular, in terms of the general, and touch abstract and concrete in the same flight of thought. He must study the present in the light of the past for the purposes of the future. No part of man's nature or his institutions must be entirely outside his regard. He must be purposeful and disinterested in a spontaneous mood, as aloof and incorruptible as an artist, yet sometimes as near to earth as a politician.[5]

Smith succinctly summarises many of the functions of the innovator: that person with that breadth of attention so as to be able to 'connect the dots' and produce combinatorial novelty – the very substance of innovation.

BOOM Costa Del Sol, Malaga, Spain, due for completion in 2014
this page and opposite: BOOM is a contemporary project in Spain offering homes for 'people who live life the way they want'. Catering for a lesbian, gay, bisexual and transgender (LGBT) community aged 40 upwards, architects including HWKN, Architensions, Dosmasuno, Nigel Coates, L2 Tsionov-Vitkon, Limon Lab, Escher GuneWardena, Messana O'Rorke and Rudin Donner fully embrace social groups that traditionally have not been catered for, reflecting a repositioning for design innovation away from conventional community expectations.

So the institutional challenge is how we can reinvent the polymath or architects of design who can rise above the constraints of disciplinary or professional blinkers. The answer lies in the support of multilingual competencies and the ability to have conversations across boundaries. The challenge for our institutions is how we might develop and support Vitruvian and Keynesian practitioners.

The contemporary innovation challenge to combine breadth and depth could – and should – prompt a revitalised appreciation of the syncretic character of architecture as a profession and the coordinating or combinatorial function of design.

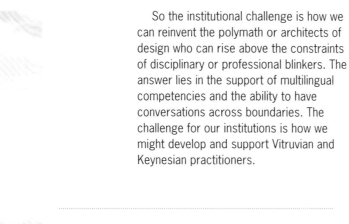

Boundary crossing raises the vexed issue of collaboration. Collaboration, like innovation, is deemed to be a good thing. We talk about and invoke the virtue of collaboration endlessly, without remarking on the fact that real and productive collaboration is extraordinarily rare and very hard work. It is antithetical to our specialisations and so the basic challenge for innovators is how to assume the role of organising collective action.

It is instructive that the English language has not produced an indigenous word to describe the innovator. We borrowed 'entrepreneur' from the French. For a while, however, it was touch and go whether or not we might preference the Italian term for innovator as 'impresario'. The impresario is the producer who pulls together a 'motley crew', to use the colourful phrase adopted by Richard Caves to describe production in the creative industries,[6] and 'puts the show on the road'. The impresario accurately describes the function and character of the innovator. An impresario easily and naturally becomes synonymous with architect or designer.

The contemporary innovation challenge to combine breadth and depth could – and should – prompt a revitalised appreciation of the syncretic character of architecture as a profession and the coordinating or combinatorial function of design. ⅃

Notes
1. Joseph Schumpeter, *Capitalism, Socialism and Democracy*, Harper (New York), 1975 [originally published 1942], pp 82–5.
2. Adam Smith, *An Inquiry into the Nature and Causes of the Wealth of Nations*, eds R Campbell, A Skinner and W Todd, Clarendon Press Edition (Oxford), 1976.
3. Smith, op cit, Book I.i.9, p 21.
4. Vitruvius, *The Ten Books on Architecture*, trans Morris Hicky Morgan, Harvard University Press (Cambridge, MA), 1914, p 6.
5. Quoted by Robert Skidelsky in *Keynes: The Return of the Master*, Allen Lane (London), 2009, p 56
6. Richard Caves, *Creative Industries: Contracts Between Art and Commerce*, Harvard University Press (Cambridge, MA), 2000.

Antoine Picon

ARCHITECTURE, INNOVATION AND TRADITION

Antoine Picon, Professor of the History of Architecture and Technology at Harvard Graduate School of Design (GSD), and the author of a significant new book, *Ornament: The Politics of Architecture and Subjectivity* (John Wiley & Sons), publishing in April 2013, provides the counterargument to this issue. He argues that for innovation to go beyond the superficial level of being a mere design trend or fashion, it needs to avoid 'presentism' and develop a reflexive stance to history and tradition.

The first diesel engine (also known as the Third Augsburg prototype), 1896–7
At this early stage of its development, the diesel engine still appears as an invention rather than a fully fledged innovation.

In technology and economics, experts usually distinguish between 'invention' and 'innovation' by contrasting the new as a mere singularity, with newness as a spreading phenomenon that changes entire fields of practice. When German engineer Thomas Diesel imagined at the end of the 19th century an engine in which ignition was triggered by pressure, he was not yet facing an innovation, but an invention the fate of which was not yet decided.[1] Despite their ingenuity, many inventions do not diffuse for reasons such as technical limitations, socio-economic and cultural obstacles. From Thomas Alva Edison's electric lighting to Malcolm McLean's containers and their special cranes and ships, innovation possesses a systemic character that involves solving multiple compatibility issues within the technology itself, developing an appropriate business model, and finding support among broad constituencies.[2]

While retaining this systemic dimension, the guest-editors of this issue of △ rightly point out the inadequacy of the general approach to technological innovation in the domain of design. Their alternative model of innovation as a generator of vitality appears intriguing. It is worth noting its strong organicist connotation. Interestingly, this organic inspiration seems not so much Darwinian, like so many neo-evolutionist theories of technological change, as Ruskinian, with its appeal to a mix of vital impulse and ethical concerns – a 'creative collective force' that presents a strong analogy with the spiritual inspiration invoked by the author of *The Seven Lamps of Architecture* (1849) and *The Stones of Venice* (1851–3).[3] This shift definitely owes something to the perspectives offered by digital culture in architecture. As Lars Spuybroek's recent book reminds us, John Ruskin's views on questions ranging from the role of nature as a source of inspiration to the importance of craftsmanship, and from ornament to ethics, echo those held by many contemporary digital designers.[4] The environmental dimension of design innovation that ranks among the themes of this issue is also present in the writing of the 19th-century theorist.

One could use this implicit lineage to challenge some of the assumptions made in the name of the 'innovation imperative'. Organicism is always risky in that it tries to identify permanent natural features without paying sufficient attention to what is actually socially constructed within nature. Instead of being a genuine natural characteristic, emergence could very well rank among such social constructs, and this would explain its current appeal.[5] As Bruno Latour has convincingly argued, are we even sure that something like a pure untouched nature lies outside the human realm as an uncharted continent waiting to be discovered?[6] However, this is not the path that will be followed here. Accepting the premises of the guest-editors – the existence of an innovation imperative that feeds today on digital and biological technologies – an additional characterisation of what true innovation means in architecture, namely a reflexive stance on history and tradition, will be proposed. Such a stance constitutes one of the prerequisites of long-term design innovation. Without it, architectural change remains at the level of superficial trend and fashion.

Although the past decades have been marked by a strong tendency to neglect historical references (Rem Koolhaas' 1978 *Delirious New York* was probably among the last major theoretical contributions by a practising architect to be based on a creative mobilisation of historical references), such presentism cannot go on

John Ruskin, Abstract Lines, plate from *The Stones of Venice*, Vol 1, 1851
For Ruskin, abstract lines, derived from nature, are the first constituents of ornament. The plate shows various lines at very different scales, from the profile of a glacier in the Alps (ab) to the curve of a branch of spruce (h). His sensitivity to the dynamic behaviour of natural elements seems to announce today's interest in flows, variations and modulations. More generally, Ruskin's work appears in tune with many concerns expressed by contemporary designers.

Studio 505, Pixel building, Melbourne, 2010
Pixel is Australia's first carbon-neutral office building.
The coloured panels provide light and control glare.
Made of recycled materials, they are supported
by spandrels that provide shading and grey-water
treatment. The project is emblematic of the close
association between ornament and environment-
friendly envelope performativity that characterises
many contemporary design approaches.

forever.[7] In fact, there are growing signs of the return of historical consciousness, one of the most striking being Patrik Schumacher's attempt to connect parametricism to the entire history of architecture and architectural thinking, from Vitruvius to Gottfried Semper, and from Gian Lorenzo Bernini to Le Corbusier.[8] Although disputable, because of its excessive ambition, such enterprise may be interpreted as a symptom of a return of history in the very domain that until now has proved particularly oblivious to it: digital architecture.[9]

But why are history and historical consciousness so important? The answer perhaps lies in the strong self-referential character of the architectural discipline. From the Renaissance to the end of the 18th century, at the time when the doctrine of imitation still prevailed in the arts, theorists often remarked that whereas painting and sculpture imitate nature, architecture had a propensity to imitate itself. Architecture is partly based on the meditation of its former achievements as well as its shortcomings. Modernism did not break with this self-reflexive stance, and now modern architecture itself has become a legacy that must be reinvested with new meaning.

In the case of architecture, self-referentiality does not mean that external conditions do not matter; to the contrary. The relation to the past represents in reality a convenient way for architectural design to open itself to the challenges of the present without becoming trapped by its limitations. To be aware of its legacy makes design more receptive to the unforeseeable future that true innovation entails. It appears as the necessary stabiliser that makes the passage from mere novelty to widespread change – from invention to innovation – possible in the field of design.

Another way to understand the role of history is to recognise that architecture is as much a tradition as a discipline. A tradition, a living tradition that is, is not something static. At each stage it implies transmission, but also a series of reinterpretations as well as abandons, the price to pay for innovation. To be effective, innovation requires at least a change of perspective, often a more drastic departure from the existing state of things. Sometimes a dimension considered as constitutive of the theory and practice can become rapidly obsolete while others are maintained and even accentuated. At other times, long-forsaken or at least neglected aspects can be retrieved or reinvented. Both scenarios have applied to ornament: it almost disappeared during the first decades of the 20th century following Adolf Loos' scathing attacks regarding its 'criminal' character,[10] but is now making a surprising return. A historical perspective is necessary to understand fully what is at stake in this revival. Again, tradition is never static. It lives through constant handing down, reinvention and loss. Ornament offers precious insight into the close relation between tradition and innovation.

What is returning is not ornament as we knew it. Contemporary architectural decor differs from what ornament used to mean on a series of key points. From the Renaissance to the end of the 19th century, ornament, at least within Western architectural tradition, used to be local, concentrated in specific points of a building such as pediments. However, it now represents a pervasive condition often affiliated only with surface. Ornament used to be added to constructive parts. In fact, it was supposed to be all the more essential to architecture in that it could be easily taken away, peeled, thus following the logic of 'supplement' analysed by Jacques Derrida in his various writings.[11] Apparently added following

an afterthought, the supplement can often reveal an inner truth masked by more structural features, just like make-up or well-chosen fashion accessories can express feelings deeper than those that words can convey. Whether built-in, carved or extruded, today's ornament is generally inseparable from the facade that it animates, so that it can no longer be removed.

What is actually returning through what we call 'ornament' is a series of concerns and questions that present a direct link with technological developments, from the new possibilities offered by the computer (contemporary ornament appears as an offspring of digital culture in architecture) to the various research regarding building envelopes in relation to the quest for sustainability. A series of broader issues including the relation between architecture, subjectivity and politics is also returning.[12] Innovation in architecture could be defined through the interaction between formal change, technological challenges and cultural concerns. In such a perspective, contemporary ornament represents an evident vector of innovation.

In addition to the ethical dimension, ornament enables us to identify another imperative at work in architectural innovation, that of making sense. Until now, digital designers have shown a tendency to discard the question of meaning as if absolutely irrelevant to an architectural decor supposed to induce only affects.[13] Is this belated reaction to Postmodernism and its abuse of gratuitous symbols still tenable? While Postmodernist solutions are still criticised, some of the issues they raise are now regaining momentum. Meaning, or rather the desire to address, in one way or another, the realm of signification and knowledge, is probably among these returning issues. Architectural innovation should not only be ethical; it must make sense. ⌂

Notes
1. Donald E Thomas, Jr, *Diesel: Technology and Society in Industrial Germany*, University of Alabama Press (Tuscaloosa, AL), 1987.
2. See, for instance, Marc Levinson, *The Box: How the Shipping Container Made the World Smaller and the World Economy Bigger*, Princeton University Press (Princeton, NJ), 2006, and Thomas P Hughes, *Networks of Power: Electrification in Western Society 1880–1930*, Johns Hopkins University Press (Baltimore, MD), 1983.
3. John Ruskin, *The Seven Lamps of Architecture*, John Wiley (New York), 1849, and *The Stones of Venice*, Smith Elder and Co (London), 1851–3.
4. Lars Spuybroek, *The Sympathy of Things: Ruskin and the Ecology of Design*, V2 Publishing (Rotterdam), 2011.
5. Michael Weinstock, *The Architecture of Emergence: The Evolution of Form in Nature and Civilisation*, John Wiley & Sons (Chichester), 2010.
6. Bruno Latour, *We Have Never Been Modern*, Harvard University Press (Cambridge, MA), 1992.
7. Rem Koolhaas, *Delirious New York: A Retroactive Manifesto for Manhattan*, Oxford University Press (New York), 1978.
8. Patrik Schumacher, *The Autopoiesis of Architecture I: A New Framework for Architecture and II: A New Agenda for Architecture*, John Wiley & Sons (London), 2011–12.
9. On the difficult relations between digital culture, history and memory, see Antoine Picon, *Digital Culture in Architecture: An Introduction for the Design Professions*, Birkhäuser (Basel), 2010.
10. Adolf Loos, 'Ornament and Crime', 1929, republished in Adolf Loos, *Ornament and Crime: Selected Essays*, Ariadne Press (Riverside, CA), 1998, pp 167–76.
11. See, for instance, Jacques Derrida, *Of Grammatology*, Paris, 1967; English translation John Hopkins University Press (Baltimore, MD), 1976.
12. Antoine Picon, *Ornament: The Politics of Architecture*, John Wiley & Sons (Chichester), 2013.
13. See Farshid Moussavi and Michael Kubo, *The Function of Ornament*, Actar (Barcelona), 2006.

Another way to understand the role of history is to recognise that architecture is as much a tradition as a discipline. A tradition, a living tradition that is, is not something static. At each stage it implies transmission, but also a series of reinterpretations as well as abandons, the price to pay for innovation.

Ruy Klein, *Klex 1*, New York, 2008
opposite: This CNC-milled high-density foam finished in pearl Chromalusion of this installation offers a striking example of the new possibilities of ornamentation through digital modeling and fabrication. The result possesses a strong organic connotation. It appears simultaneously reminiscent of the intricacies of Islamic and Gothic vaults, not to mention Antoni Gaudi's architecture.

Mario Carpo teaches architectural history and theory at the School of Architecture at Yale University and at the École d'Architecture de Paris-La Villette. His research and publications focus on the relationship between architectural theory, cultural history, and the history of media and information technology. His *Architecture in the Age of Printing* (MIT Press, 2001) has been translated into several languages. His most recent books are *The Alphabet and the Algorithm* (MIT Press, 2011), a history of digital design theory, and *The Digital Turn in Architecture, 1992–2012*, an Đ Reader.

Oron Catts is the co-founder and director of SymbioticA: the Centre of Excellence in Biological Arts at the University of Western Australia (UWA), and a visiting professor of design interaction at the Royal College of Art, London. **Ionat Zurr**, who received her PhD from the Faculty of Architecture, Landscape and Visual Arts, UWA, is a researcher and SymbioticA's academic coordinator. Both are currently visiting professors at *BiofiliA* Base for Biological Arts at Aalto University, Helsinki. Catts and Zurr are artists, researchers and curators, and formed the internationally renowned Tissue Culture & Art Project. They have been artists in residence at UWA's School of Anatomy, Physiology and Human Biology since 1996, and were central to the establishment of SymbioticA in 2000. They are considered pioneers in the field of biological arts and are invited as keynote speakers, curate exhibitions, publish widely, and exhibit internationally. Their work is in the collection of the Museum of Modern Art

(MoMA), New York, and they have recently had a retrospective show in Poland.

Terry Cutler is an Australia-based industry consultant and strategy advisor with a background in the information and communications technology sector. He has authored numerous influential reports and papers on the digital economy and innovation. During 2008 he chaired the Australian government's Review of the National Innovation System, which culminated in the report *Venturous Australia*. He is a Fellow of the Australian Academy of Technological Sciences and Engineering, the Australian Academy of the Humanities, and the Australian Institute of Public Administration. In 2003 he was awarded Australia's Centenary Medal.

Tom Daniell is a practising architect and academic based in Japan. He is currently head of the architecture programme at the University of St Joseph in Macau, Visiting Associate Professor at the University of Hong Kong, Visiting Fellow at the RMIT Spatial Information Architecture Lab (SIAL), and Adjunct Professor at Victoria University of Wellington. Widely published, he is an editorial consultant for the journals *Mark*, *Volume* and *Interstices*. His books include *FOBA: Buildings* (Princeton Architectural Press, 2005), *After the Crash: Architecture in Post-Bubble Japan* (Princeton Architectural Press, 2008), *Houses and Gardens of Kyoto* (Tuttle Shokai Inc, 2010), and *Kiyoshi Sey Takeyama + Amorphe* (Equal Books, 2011).

Eva Franch i Gilabert is the founder of OOAA (office of architectural affairs) and the director of Storefront for Art and Architecture. Her work occupies the practice of architecture through building, curating, drawing, teaching and writing. She holds a Master of Architecture from ETSA Barcelona-UPC and a MArch II from Princeton University.

Jondi Keane is an arts practitioner, critical thinker and senior lecturer at Deakin University, Australia. Over the last 30 years he has exhibited and performed in the US, UK, Europe and Australia, focusing on interdisciplinary and collaborative installation performances. He has published in a range of journals and edited collections on embodiment and embodied cognition, the philosophy of perception, experimental architecture, research design and practice-led research.

Greg Lynn has received a Golden Lion at the Venice Biennale of Architecture and the American Academy of Arts & Letters Architecture Award; he was also awarded a fellowship from United States Artists. *Time* magazine named him one of the 100 most innovative people in the world for the 21st century, and *Forbes* magazine named him one of the 10 most influential living architects. He graduated from Miami University of Ohio with Bachelor of Environmental Design and Bachelor of Philosophy degrees, and from Princeton University with a Master of Architecture. He is the author of seven books.

Brian Massumi is a professor in the Communication Department of the University of Montreal. He is the author of *Semblance and Event: Activist Philosophy and the Occurrent Arts* (MIT Press, 2011); *Parables for the Virtual: Movement, Affect, Sensation* (Duke University Press, 2002); *A User's Guide to Capitalism and Schizophrenia: Deviations from Deleuze and Guattari* (MIT Press, 1992); and (with Kenneth Dean) *First and Last Emperors: The Absolute State and the Body of the Despot* (Autonomedia, 1993). His translations from the French include Gilles Deleuze and Félix Guattari's *A Thousand Plateaus*.

Antoine Picon is Professor of the History of Architecture and Technology and Co-Director of Doctoral Programs at Harvard Graduate School of Design (GSD). He has published numerous books and articles mostly dealing with the complementary histories of architecture and technology, among which are: *French Architects and Engineers in the Age of Enlightenment* (Cambridge University Press, 2009); *Claude Perrault (1613–1688) ou la curiosité d'un classique* (Délégation à l'action artistique de la ville de Paris, 1988); *L'Invention de L'ingénieur moderne, L'Ecole des Ponts et Chaussées 1747–1851* (Presses de l'Ecole nationale des ponts et chausses, 1992); *La ville territoire des cyborgs* (Verdier, 1999); and *Digital Culture in Architecture: An Introduction for the Design Professions* (Birkhäuser, 2010). His new book on the contemporary return of ornament in architecture, entitled *Ornament: The Politics of Architecture and Subjectivity* (John Wiley & Sons), is publishing in April 2013.

Veronika Valk is an architect in her practice Zizi&Yoyo, a board member of the Kultuurikatel NGO, and a tutor at the Estonian Academy of Arts, from which she graduated in 2001. She has also studied at the Rhode Island School of Design, and is currently a PhD candidate at RMIT University School of Architecture and Design. She has won some 30 prizes in architecture, design and urban-planning competitions, and has published a number of articles on architecture and urbanism.

Leon van Schaik AO is Professor of Architecture (Innovation Chair) at RMIT. He has promoted local and international architectural culture through design practice research and commissioning. Publications include *Mastering Architecture: Becoming a Creative Innovator in Practice* (2005), *Design City Melbourne* (2006) and *Spatial Intelligence* (2008), all published by John Wiley & Sons, as well as *Denton Corker Marshall: Non-Fictional Narratives* (Birkhäuser, 2008), *Procuring Innovative Architecture*, with Geoffrey London and Beth George (Routledge, 2010) and *Meaning in Space: Housing the Visual Arts, or Architectures for Private Collections* (LHM, 2012).

Michael Weinstock is an architect, and currently Director of Research and Development, and founder and director of the Emergent Technologies and Design programme in the Graduate School of the Architectural Association (AA) School of Architecture in London. He studied at the AA from 1982 to 1988 and has taught since 1989 in a range of positions from workshop tutor through to academic head. He has published and lectured widely on the forms and dynamics of natural systems, and the application of their mathematics and processes to cities, to groups of buildings within cities, and to individual buildings. Current research focuses on the 'flow architectures' of urban metabolisms that are intimately coupled to the spatial and cultural patterns of life in the city, to the public spaces through which people flow, and that integrate morphological, ecological and cultural systems.

Gretchen Wilkins is a Senior Lecturer in Architecture at RMIT University, where she coordinates the Urban Architecture Laboratory and is acting Program Director for the Master of Urban Design programme. She is the editor of *Distributed Urbanism: Cities After Google Earth* (Routledge, 2010), *Entropia: Incremental Gestures Towards a Possible Urbanism* (Champ Libre, 2008) and *On-The-Spot: Atelier Hitoshi Abe* (University of Michigan, 2007).

What is *Architectural Design*?

Founded in 1930, *Architectural Design* (△) is an influential and prestigious publication. It combines the currency and topicality of a newsstand journal with the rigour and production qualities of a book. With an almost unrivalled reputation worldwide, it is consistently at the forefront of cultural thought and design.

Each title of △ is edited by an invited guest-editor, who is an international expert in the field. Renowned for being at the leading edge of design and new technologies, △ also covers themes as diverse as architectural history, the environment, interior design, landscape architecture and urban design.

Provocative and inspirational, △ inspires theoretical, creative and technological advances. It questions the outcome of technical innovations as well as the far-reaching social, cultural and environmental challenges that present themselves today.

For further information on △, subscriptions and purchasing single issues see: www.architectural-design-magazine.com

How to Subscribe

With 6 issues a year, you can subscribe to △ (either print, online or through the △ App for iPad).

INSTITUTIONAL SUBSCRIPTION
£212/US$398 print or online

INSTITUTIONAL SUBSCRIPTION
£244/US$457 combined print & online

PERSONAL-RATE SUBSCRIPTION
£120/US$189 print and iPad access

STUDENT-RATE SUBSCRIPTION
£75/US$117 print only

To subscribe to print or online:
Tel: +44 (0) 1243 843 272
Email: cs-journals@wiley.com

△ APP FOR iPAD
For information on the △ App for iPad go to www.architectural-design-magazine.com
6-issue subscription: £44.99/US$64.99
Individual issue: £9.99/US$13.99

Volume 82 No 1
ISBN 978 1119 993780

Volume 82 No 2
ISBN 978 0470 973301

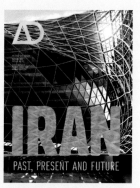

Volume 82 No 3
ISBN 978 1119 974505

Volume 82 No 4
ISBN 978 1119 973621

Volume 82 No 5
ISBN 978 1119 972662

Volume 82 No 6
ISBN 978 1118 336410